It Wasnae Me!

A Personal Account of Childhood and Adolescence in 1950s and 1960s

Scotland.

By JP Glynn

All family names have been changed.

For Evelyn, Sylvia, Bill, Desmond and Eileen

Contents

Introduction

Forty years after leaving Scotland to live in Sheffield England, I came across a book written by a man who re-called his childhood and adolescence as part of a working class family in that city, during the second half of the 1940s and the 1950s.

His recollections inspired me to record my own experiences of life as a child and young adult in a working class family, during the two decades following World War 2. While there are many similarities, "It Wasnae Me" chronicles events from *my* childhood and adolescence, that took place in the vastly different setting of Bannockburn, a small, country town in an historic part of Scotland.

There are a number of literary records giving individual accounts of childhood during wars or economic depressions. They were sometimes funny sometimes sad, very often humbling and to me, hugely interesting. The following account however, tells the tale of growing up during a period when the population were dusting off the doom and gloom of war. The young people who had 'lived for today because we might be dead tomorrow', were now parents themselves, and had high hopes and expectations of a peaceful and prosperous future for their children.

It contains the personal trials and tribulations of my own childhood and adolescence, within a family of mixed uncaring relatives, whilst focusing on the social attitudes and cultural activities of a small town community in Scotland throughout the 1950s and 1960s. I hope it will offer generations who follow an insight to childhood and adolescence during those decades.

Religion played a huge part in my life throughout those years. Religious influences along with some of the traditions I once held dear, now appear to have been unnecessary trivialities. The schools I attended were excellent. The dedicated staff, wide range of subjects, and my fellow pupils combined to make school life a very happy time for me.

In sharp contrast to within our house, outside the home is where I was happiest. The schools, streets where I hung around, the beautiful park and woods where I played alongside my friends and cousins from my extended family, were all places where I felt happy, free, and safe. Playtimes were always fun and exciting, with plenty to keep young imaginations occupied before the advent of Television. Outings to seaside resorts besides local beauty spots provided welcome changes for our adventures. Like most small communities, it also had an array of colourful characters and authoritative figures.

Commentators have said that if you can remember the '60s then you were not there. Well I *was* there and I *do* remember, though my memories are perhaps, not typical. In 1969, aged 19, I found the courage to spread my wings to become mistress of my own destiny. The most important decision I had made so far, took me on the journey into England where I continue to live.

The 1950s and 1960s, was a period when technology had not yet become the popular method for retaining historical records. Therefore, the availability of written accounts by observers who were present at that time, will give a broader perspective to our descendants. At the same time though, I hope my account will offer my peers a few nostalgic glimpses of their own childhood, so perhaps they too, will be inspired to record their experiences of that era.

However questionable the morals of the post-war grown-ups in my immediate family, the people and beautiful surroundings of Bannockburn and the nearby town of Stirling, combined to have a deeply profound affect on me, thus shaping the person I am today. It is here where my recollections take place.

Chapter One

Beautiful Bannockburn

When asked how long I have lived in Sheffield, I usually reply, "When man landed on the moon I landed in Sheffield." The Sheffield 'landing' occurred in July 1969, as did the moon landing. I was a very naive 19 year old embarking on a journey from the God fearing country of Scotland, to a new life in God's own county of Yorkshire, England. Of course my response revealed a Scottish accent which would then bring about the question "Oh, do you come from Glasgow then?" My only connection with Glasgow is that I was born and baptized there. At around the age of three, I was taken to live with my maternal grandmother in the small rural historic town of Bannockburn, which lays around 26 miles north east of Glasgow, around 27 miles north west of Edinburgh, and three miles south of Stirling.

Bannockburn of the 1950s was a beautiful town. It would not be an exaggeration to describe it as a child's Utopia. Luscious green parks and woodlands to play in, alongside a relatively young housing development, were in my opinion, the nicest and safest places on earth. However picturesque the physical surroundings of my childhood home may have been, the atmosphere within the four walls of the house where I grew up was in stark contrast. A domineering, uncaring aunt along with her bullying son was quite frightening for a child. I took solace however, from the kindness and love shown to me by my cousin and my brother, until that is, they left home.

The time I spent in Glasgow was brief but, it seems to me, anyone who announced they came from Scotland via Glasgow is widely believed to have lived in a huge Tenement building, in a run down part of the city called The Gorbals. Tenements were huge residential buildings sometimes with three, four or more storeys. They had only the most basic amenities and housed a large number of families, some of whom lived in overcrowded situations. Furthermore, they had a reputation for squalid living conditions where many children had no green safe areas in which to play. Most are demolished, but around the 1950s they were home to many, whom I am sure, like me, have happy and sad memories in equal quantity.

Besides having its share of large cities with run down areas, Scotland in the 1950s had numerous lovely small rural towns and Bannockburn at that time was just such a town. Here we were cocooned in our own five square miles of blissful paradise and where I proudly announce to enquirers, was my hometown.

Bannockburn Childrens Playground, Bannockburn, Scotland 1950's.

Throughout my adolescence the larger town of Stirling three miles away played a huge part too. For hundreds of years it was a Royal Borough then, in 2002 to celebrate Queen Elizabeth's Golden Jubilee it was granted City status. It stands on the River Forth, which meanders east into the Firth of Forth and beyond Scotland's capital Edinburgh. The city's main focal point is its ancient castle, which sits upon a high crag and commands magnificent views. The Ochil Hills lay to the east, the Campsie Fells to the west and the Grampian Mountains in the distance to the north. It is easy to see why Stirling is regarded by many, as the gateway to the Highlands.

This proud medieval fortress stands high in the town, defiantly facing south overlooking the road to England. It is embraced by the crab-like pincers of the aforementioned hills and mountains, as if to protect the town from would-be invaders. The Wallace monument stands on a crag opposite Stirling Castle and it too faces south. It was erected to the memory of Sir William Wallace, Scotland's enigmatic hero and famous freedom fighter. The top of the Wallace monument commands, in my opinion one of the most breathtakingly beautiful views in the whole of the United Kingdom. The main road to Glasgow and the south west of Scotland runs through the west side of Bannockburn, whilst towards the east runs the main road to

Edinburgh and the south east of Scotland. It is the east side where I lived in a close-knit community within my maternal extended family.

Our immediate neighbourhood was a relatively small one and consisted of three streets called Park Crescent, Park Drive, and Park Gardens, collectively known as Park Crescent. These streets consisted of beautiful three and four bedroom two storey, white painted pebble-dashed houses. Some were semi-detached, whilst others were in rows of four and it was around these streets where I spent my childhood and youth.

The local authorities built the houses in the 1930s and my maternal grandparents had been amongst their first inhabitants. Each house had its own indoor bathroom, gardens to the front and rear, electricity, an open fireplace in every room and a black lead cooking range in the kitchen that also heated a large tank for hot water. According to chronicles of the living conditions of many towns and cities in the 1930s, these must have seemed luxurious. These houses have certainly stood the test of time because, around 70 years later they are still in excellent condition, many of the residents are owner/occupiers and a number of my grandparents great grandchildren still live there.

The open fields belonging to Mr. Miller the local farmer ran alongside our three streets and formed part of the northern boundary between

Bannockburn and Stirling. Although nearby St. Ninians and Stirling were clearly visible in the distance, we did not venture into these towns until we were older. A five-minute walk south from Park Crescent and beyond Mr. & Mrs Miller's farm, took us to a huge play park, which was surely created by God himself. It looked as if he had gathered a giant mound of green grass, surrounded it by trees, then took a huge spoon and scooped out the middle. He then made about 30 wooden steps to enable us to reach the bottom where there were swings, and other playground rides along with a paddling pool, which was a wonderful attraction in summer.

Many families would bring a picnic and the mums sat on a raised grassy area while the children splashed and played in the pool. This may seem nothing out of the ordinary in those days, but what were out of the ordinary were the two streams that flowed through the park. One was a small and very shallow rivulet where younger children could paddle on a hot day or catch tiny minnow fish; sadly, it is now dried up and overgrown with grass and blends in with the rest of the huge grassy expanse. Nearby, an old monkey puzzle tree hung over this stream, which provided great tree climbing practice for us would-be Tarzans and Janes. The other is the River Bannock from where the town takes its name. It flows under the high road bridge that carries the main road to Edinburgh and was a wonderful place for older children to scramble around its rocky bed, particularly when the water was at its lowest. After heavy rainfall however, it becomes treacherous and just the angry roar and speed of the water deterred us from going near it on such days. Whilst on a visit there when my own children were young, the memory of this compelled me to take hold of their hands and pull them back from the waters edge, even though it was a calm sunny day and the water was relatively shallow.

Given the area's history of battles it is no wonder the river can sometimes sound so angry. Historians have recorded there were so many bodies laying in the waters of the River Bannock after the Battle of Bannockburn in 1314, that King Robert the Bruce's men did not get their feet wet crossing it whilst rousting the surviving English King Edward's soldiers from the battlefield.

Following the footpath eastward and parallel to the river, through fields and scrubland for about half a mile, we came to the bridge, which carried the railway line from the south to Stirling and the Highlands beyond. We named it the thunder bridge because of the thunderous noise made by the trains as they passed over. The river was shallow at this point and we spent many happy hours underneath the bridge fishing for minnows or just paddling around. It was at this spot where we would put stones on the railway line and watch the sparks fly when the trains' wheels went over them. Beyond the bridge was an area named the clay hole, sometimes called the bog. This was usually out of bounds for us smaller children as it was an open area with a huge reservoir of water. It is believed that around the turn of the 20th century, a working quarry was here. However I can re-call my older brother and his friends swimming in there and generally having a good time. This formed an eastern boundary for us and the adjoining northern boundary was a short distance through a couple of fields to the bluebell wood. Named thus for obvious reasons it was situated near St. Mary's primary school and was a great place to build dens or hides. Loose branches and hedges along with mossy bracken, made an impregnable castle which Robert the Bruce himself would have had trouble capturing. The hedgerows grew an abundance of Brambles, or Blackberries, so we never ran out of food supplies. Besides these food supplies, there was a shallow fresh water spring nearby which combined to sustain us throughout our hard fought battles. There are conflicting theories amongst historians regarding the actual site of the battle, and the Bluebell Wood/Park Crescent area is a hot favourite.

Although the carpet of bluebells was glorious in the spring, they hid a dangerous boggy marsh, which we had to negotiate very carefully if we were to avoid getting stuck ankle deep, or even sinking, in the mud. Many a child had gone home minus a shoe or sometimes a pair of shoes because of a misplaced step. Some of the trees in the wood were situated on a very steep slope, which provided an ideal place for a homemade swing. A good length of strong rope tied around the centre of a thick 2ft. length of wood and we were soon transported from a medieval castle to the jungles of Africa and the home of Jane and her hero Tarzan.

During one of our escapades in the bluebell woods I regretfully, had a go at playing Jane on the rope swing whilst wearing a skirt. When it was time to let someone else have a go, I began to unravel my legs from off the swing but unfortunately for me, my skirt decided to stay put. Moreover, as I was frantically trying to untangle the skirt from around it whilst standing on tiptoe, my skirt head high, I suddenly felt a hand on my back pushing me forward. There I was, dangling in mid-air with my friends, boys as well as girls, almost splitting their sides with laughter at the sight of me twirling around with my knickers on display. When I managed to get free, my skirt was torn all across the front. Everyone present took off any badges or pins that they had on them, to hold the skirt together, so I could walk through the streets and back home with what little dignity I had left. I never attempted swinging again whilst wearing a skirt.

Due to the steep incline in the play area of the park, it was known locally as the bottom park. When we crossed the bridge over the river, climbed upwards through the trees by way of a number of winding wooden steps, we reached the aptly named top park. About halfway up the incline was what could be described as a mini lagoon, a pool of fresh water which was filled by a natural spring winding down the hill, which then carried on to join the river below. This was a wonderful oasis for us kids, after all playing, fighting battles and climbing trees were thirsty work. The water tasted brilliant, pure nectar in fact. It was common practice after a picnic, to take our empty bottles of Scotland's favourite fizzy drink 'Irn Bru', and fill them with the water to sustain us throughout yet more adventures. Around 25yrs later, I took my daughters to fill the aforementioned bottles with this nectar and it tasted just as I remembered it. Sadly, it has since dried up, but I have often wondered if I am now buying in supermarkets, the best tasting, most pure water found anywhere, that was once free.

The top park area had like the bottom park, swings, a roundabout, and a huge grassy area. The town's monument to the local men who were killed in the two world wars stood here. I was always proud to point out my cousin's name engraved there, who had been killed in World War 2 five years before I was born. He was the first of two illegitimate sons of my aunt Betty and had been an R.A.F. Bomber Pilot Officer. When the parks daffodils were in bloom and unknown to my elders, I used to pick, or I really should say steal a bunch, and take them the few hundred yards to Bannockburn cemetery and place them on his grave. During one of these flower laying ceremonies, the graveyard caretaker stopped me to ask where I got them. I replied that my mum gave them to me and told me to put them on my uncle's grave. As a catholic, I was very uncomfortable with this lie, so I blessed myself with the sign of the cross and made a silent promise to confess my sin to Father McAlister at my next confession.

An exit gate from the top park would find us on the main street of Bannockburn. 'Up the toon' as it was locally known, had a variety of shops, along with a cinema, police station, three churches, three pubs, the library, and Bannockburn Public Primary School. Besides serving Park Crescent and the wider community, these amenities served homes at the top of the town too. The main road to Edinburgh continued south out of town, but this shopping area and particularly the school, formed the southern boundary for our playtime expeditions.

Across the main Edinburgh road and opposite Park Crescent, is a sprawling housing complex known as Hillpark. With similar but fewer amenities to that at the top of the town, it lays between the main roads to Glasgow and Edinburgh. Its top most part continued up to the busy Glasgow road thereby forming the western boundary for our explorations.

Chapter Two

The Family

I was born in Glasgow Scotland in 1949, the third child of a woman who already had two illegitimate children that were born during the war years, Patrick and Philomena. I, on the other hand, was legitimate but nonetheless, never knew my father and had only a vague knowledge of my mother. From birth until around the age of three, I had been part of a family of eight children. Our mother Morag, had married a widower with five children, and along with her own two illegitimate children, settled in Glasgow. I was the only product of that marriage. When the marriage failed around three years after I was born, I was separated from my father and half siblings, and was never told of their existence. Throughout my entire childhood and adolescence, I had been led to believe that my half brother and half sister were my only siblings and that both our parents were dead. Neither parent was involved in my upbringing because, in the early 1950s, my two siblings and I went to live with relatives at our mother's childhood home 26 miles away.

Throughout the 14 years or so that I lived at this house, it was made clear to me that I was most unwelcome, therefore I was sometimes unhappy, and often lonely and afraid. The feelings of loneliness were exacerbated when it became clear that I had a different surname from everyone else in my large extended family, including that of my siblings. The saying "You can be lonely in a crowd" rang true for me. Moreover, there were a number of family secrets and lies that, had I known the truth about at the time, may have made life tolerable.

Immediately after she took me, Patrick and Philomena to Bannockburn, mother left to resume her life back in Glasgow. I was around three or four years old at the time, therefore I do not have any memories of her. Some years later, Philomena told me that I had been placed in a children's home, but my granny had objected and insisted I was brought to her house to be with my two siblings. I have not heard or seen anything to substantiate her remark, but there were moments when I had wondered if she had been correct.

It was a strange household with a mixed bag of relatives. My earliest memory is of sitting at the kitchen table while my granny was preparing food on the cooking range. In the living room there was a grandmother clock on the wall and from my vantage point in the kitchen, I could watch and listen to the soothing gentle 'tick-tock' noise of the pendulum as it swung back and forth. A few weeks after my sixth birthday, granny died, at home in her own bed. I had kissed her goodnight the night before, and when I went into her bedroom the next morning, her bed was empty. Despite my young age, I knew that my life would now change forever. Today, whenever my house is empty and quiet, the sound of my own pendulum clock takes me back to that kitchen and I can almost feel my granny's presence.

My mother's eldest sister aunty Betty, had lived in granny's house with her son George since her own divorce a number of years previously, and she now became my official carer, but I use the word 'carer' extremely loosely. About once or twice a year, someone would come from the Children's Department (the forerunner of the Social Services) to check that we were being looked after properly. Miss Patterson was a lovely, tall woman who as I re-call, always wore a headscarf. I was scared to talk to her because, before every visit, our aunt would say to us "Noo mind, if she asks ye aboot yer mammy or daddy, ye tell her thur baith deed"! An astonishing thing to say to young children, but we did as we were told, although strangely, Miss Patterson never asked us about our parents. Moreover, we never asked anyone, not even family members, where our mummy and daddy were. As with everything within the realms of this family, nothing was questioned, nor explanations offered.

Aunty Betty made every decision concerning my life, at every stage from childhood into adolescence. What I ate, what I wore, who I played with, or not played with if she didn't happen to like the family of a playmate. Even as a working girl between the ages of 15 and 17, she decided whether I could go to town or the disco, what to wear, how my hair should look, and the wearing of make-up was non-negotiable. I never found the strength nor courage to stand up for myself, although occasionally, an ill chosen comment would come spilling forth from my mouth, which inevitably led to a physical beating with the dreaded cane carpet beater. We children of the 1950's showed much respect for our elders, but the pain from that carpet beater was so deeply entrenched, that respect soon turned to fear.

George was one of two cousins who also lived at Granny's. He was the second of aunty Betty's illegitimate sons: her first son as I mentioned earlier, was killed in the war: and the product of a post divorce relationship, and a family secret for many years. George's physical and emotional cruelty matched that of his mother's, and his presence filled me with dread. He was around ten years older than I was, and never spoke to me unless it was to chastise me, either verbally or physically, and usually just for some minor annoyance. He would never ask me to fetch, or do something for him he commanded it. Of course, like all bullies, he only behaved like that when no one was around who would stand up for me. Patrick was away in the Navy and our other cousin Sheena, was married and living in a town some distance away.

Sheena was the daughter of my mother's older sister Sadie. At around 15 years older than me, she was the oldest of the children living in granny's house: Sadie was engaged when she fell pregnant, but her fiancée abandoned her. This was yet another secret that did not become manifest until many years later. Her subsequent marriage to Fergus was childless: She was my favourite and my protector, but best of all, she would not tolerate George's behaviour and could stand up to him. Aunty Sadie and uncle Fergus lived three miles away in Stirling. They were frequent, and as far as I was concerned, very welcome visitors. Along with myself, Patrick and Philomena, it meant six members of the same family with three different surnames, were living in one house. Cousin Isobel, who was the product of Betty's earlier marriage, lived nearby with her husband Jock and their large and growing family.

This was the early 1950s and only a few years since the end of the war, therefore it was not uncommon to have different surnames living at the same address. Many families around the country had to accommodate extended relatives still waiting to be re-housed because of the thousands of homes that had been destroyed by bombing during the war. In our family though, it was D for divorce rather than D for destruction, which threw us all together under one roof. No one ever uttered the word divorce, at least not within my earshot and especially not in our Catholic household. It did not help that due to my parents' marriage then subsequent divorce; yet another skeleton from the cupboard of plenty that I did not find out about until many years later; I did not have the same surname as *any* other member of the family, not even my brother and sister, though I never asked why. I do however remember feeling a sort of stigma attached to this, of being different. One of the family but not quite *part* of the family, but I was too young to truly comprehend. In those days, most children were seen and not heard, but in our house, this seemed to apply especially to me.

It soon became clear to me that Betty disliked her sister immensely, and as I bore a strong physical resemblance to my mother, extended that dislike towards me. I had overheard her say that when the three sisters were young, mother had been granddad's favourite, and since she was the brainy one of the family, she worked in an office. Betty and Sadie on the other hand worked in the local Mill. This had meant that my Grandparents made special efforts to ensure that my mother wore the best clothes, making Betty rage with jealousy. Sadie on the other hand, had a good relationship with Morag, probably infuriating Betty even more. On countless occasions, Betty would say to me "just like yer mither" in a nasty tone of voice. Her favourite phrase however was "If it wasnae' fur me ye'd be in a home" or, "You dinnae belong here". The latter comment I could not have agreed with more. However, what she failed to mention was that if it had not been for us, she could not have continued financially to live in this four bedroom house for as long as she did.

The Children's Department paid her as our foster carer, along with contributing to the cost of our clothes, so we did not live there out of the goodness of her heart but as a means of providing her with a bit of extra income. Apart from the monetary benefits, each of us became the cleaner, gardener, nurse, and general dogsbody, thus providing herself and her idle son with personal servants on tap.

The ultimate hurtful remark was that I had killed her mother, my beloved Granny. On many occasions she would say "If it wasnae fur you ma mither wid still be here" followed by "You killed ma mither"! Deep in my heart, I knew I had not because, as I said earlier, I was only around five or six years old at the time. I never asked aunty Betty why she accused me of such a horrible thing, but I can remember on one occasion answering back "It wasnae' me"! For many years however, agonizing questions would sometimes pop into my head, "Did I?" "Was it something I had done that caused her to die?" Perhaps I had left a toy on the floor and she had tripped over! Furthermore, despite the passing of many years and on meeting again, she never offered an apology, but I suppressed the urge to cry out aloud, "It wasnae me who killed ma' granny"!

For the first three or four years after granny died, my life in this house was relatively uneventful. Occasionally, I would have to stay overnight along the road at my cousin Isobel's house, and share a bed with three or four of her daughters, but to me this was a welcome change as I loved their company. Furthermore, Isobel and Jock always treated me like one of their own and for short spells, I felt part of a 'normal' family. However, the normality in Isobel's house was not present in our house, as the emotional and physical cruelty from Betty and George, became increasingly frightening. If my aunt's verbal cruelty was bad, her occasional physical cruelty could sometimes be worse. There were times when if either Betty or George was shouting at me, I wet myself with fear. This only led to a further scolding or slap around the face.

One summer evening when I was 15 minutes late coming home from the park, I received a thrashing with that old faithful of hers, the bamboo carpet beater. Not so much for being late, but for protesting my innocence because none of us owned a watch, so we were unable to tell what time it was. Whenever physical punishment was dished out, it was usually via this carpet beater. Even though the days of beating carpets with it had long gone, it still served the purpose of corporal punishment. I had the privilege of breaking it up some years later and throwing it in the bin. I am certain I was not the only one who was glad to see it go. However, its replacement was a long handled sweeping brush, which served the same purpose.

If all six of us were in the house at the same time in the evening, the three-piece suite could not seat everyone therefore, I sat on the floor behind one of the single chairs. This did not bother me in the least because it meant I was out of view of aunty Betty and George. Besides, it was actually quite comfortable, as has to be said for the rest of the house. My aunt had good taste in furnishings and like many others of her generation, saved to buy household goods, rather than get into debt by having items on hire purchase, or HP. This form of credit was a relatively new phenomenon *to* the working class, intended *for* the working class, but everyone regarded it with trepidation. Considering the huge amounts of debt that large numbers of individuals owe today, that generation probably had the foresight and good sense to adopt that attitude.

There was always food on the table, which usually consisted of three courses, a warm fire in the grate, and I only had to share a bed with Philomena in our own room. Along with the aforementioned help from the children's department, we were always well dressed and shod too.

The day Sheena left our house to marry Hamish, was the single most traumatic event since granny died. Any small semblance of happiness or fun that had existed in that house left with her. As she had left our house after an argument with our aunt, most of us did not attend her wedding. Only Philomena, who was her bridesmaid and aunty Sadie her mother, along with her husband uncle Fergus, represented our side of the family. However, whilst I was out playing I heard through the neighbours' gossip grapevine that the ceremony was in progress in our local church, Our Lady and St.Ninian. I ran as fast I could the half-mile or so to the church and made it in time to see her make her vows. She looked beautiful and I was missing her terribly. I cried into my pillow for many nights after she left. Quietly of course, there was no room in our house and family for displays of emotional distress.

When my peers recall their childhood bath times with their mums; along with dressing, hair washing and combing and other roles usually reserved for mothers; it is Sheena whom I recall doing these for me. It was also she who hand washed the clothes for the entire household before we acquired an electric washing machine, along with many other household chores. Moreover, she also had a full time job as manager of a shoe shop.

While she was living in the house there was laughter, fun, music and dancing, especially when she put on her rock 'n roll records and pulled Philomena and me up to dance. As I was small, it was easy for her to throw me up and around her waist, then through her legs. She would allow me to look at her lovely clothes; especially her high-heeled shoes; every pair had its own box or shoetree; give me her empty body mist deodorant spray bottles that made great water pistols, and didn't mind me generally hanging around her. The house was always clean, tidy, and warm and I had lots of freedom to go out and play with my friends in the park, woods, or the street whilst she was there. Her leaving meant that Philomena and I had to take on more chores than before. Thus, at the age of around 9 or 10 along with my sister, I had to learn to light the fire, clean the bathroom, vacuum, polish, work the washing machine, do the ironing, and every other household chore required of us.

Worst of all however, was gardening. I loathed this job because we had a large rockery, which meant moving every stone or rock to one side, pulling out the weeds, and placing the rocks back in their original position. On many evenings, Philomena and I would still be weeding in the dark, except for the street lamp, just to get the job done. Later, when my sister left home and there was only me left, I would do a section one evening and another section the next, over two or three days. My hands used to be red raw, and would sometimes bleed from sores across the knuckles. For a sixteen year old, this was very embarrassing.

Before he married Sheena, Hamish had been in the Merchant Navy, and he was just as lovely as she was. On the first Christmas Eve that I was allowed to attend midnight mass, he gave me a present of my first watch. He had bought it in the port of Antwerp Belgium. It was pink gold and it shone brilliantly. It was magnificent and I absolutely adored it. Whilst he was away at sea, Sheena took me to the cinema and other outings. It was on one of our cinema trips that I saw the musical South Pacific for the first time. Although it was a summer evening, it had begun to grow dark by the time we emerged from the cinema. I thought it was great to be in Stirling so late in the evening, but my aunt did not think so and she expressed her disapproval when we got home.

Patrick was seven years older than I was and I loved him to bits. Perhaps due to the age difference, we did not have much in common, but through unspoken words, I knew he cared for me too. He was a genuine, smashing bloke who always got on well with all the family. When he joined the navy, it was yet another trauma along with a loss of security for me. However, I loved the times when he was home on leave, and not just for the presents that he brought for me. His presence in the house again made me feel happy and safe. On Sunday mornings during his leave visits, I would make sure I was ready to leave the house for mass at the same time as him so I could walk proudly beside him in his naval uniform. Patrick and Sheena had been the only ones I could totally depend on for protection from my aunt and her son, therefore when they left home, I felt very vulnerable and insecure.

Philomena was five years older than I was and we never bonded. There were times later though, when she stood up for me, especially against George. One day George had an argument with his mother, which resulted in him moving out and going to live with his future wife, at her mother's house in another town in central Scotland. It was not until a year or so later when he brought his wife, new baby, and toddler to live with us, that his behaviour became more irrational. Then, what seemed to me to be his mission to make my life hell began to unfold. I was around 12 years old.

One evening as he sat reading with his legs stretched out into the hearth of the living room fireplace, my aunt told me to sweep up the coals and ash that had fallen out of the blazing fire. For fear of repercussions if I had asked him to move his legs, I began sweeping around them. This irritated him so much that he lifted his right foot and kicked me on my backside saying "Oh get a move on". Of course, this threw me completely off balance and sent me headlong into the fire. Luckily in a split second, I managed to lift my right arm on to the blazing coals and push myself off, falling backwards towards the floor. Thankfully, my arm was only slightly burned therefore it did not require a doctor. As my aunt was my official carer, a doctor would have been obliged to report it to the Children's Department and an investigation would have ensued. Unfortunately, I did not know or understand this at the time, indeed, if I had, action may have been taken to prevent future incidents.

What stands out more clearly in my memory of this incident was not so much the deed itself, but his complete and total lack of remorse. Moreover, when his sister and his wife who had been in the kitchen, came running in on hearing my screams, he did not look up once from his paper, even as they were giving him a good telling off. This cold brutality only intensified my fear of him, which unfortunately, was justified on later occasions. On numerous occasions, he would even bully his mother, by poking her constantly in the arm until she gave in to his demand for money until his next payday.

Philomena also suffered from his cruelty. One beautiful, hot summer day, I was chatting to his wife Fiona in the kitchen when she asked, "Why aren't you out playing with your friends?" I replied in a hushed voice "I can't, SHE won't let me", referring to aunty Betty. He must have heard because he rose from his chair, came in to the kitchen, and without uttering one word, slapped me hard across the face. As he did so, the other side of my face hit the door architrave, which caused me to cry out loudly in pain. He then calmly returned to his chair. On hearing this, my sister who had been mowing the lawn; something *he* would never dream of doing, nor his mother expect him to do; opened the living room window from outside and demanded to know what had happened. Angrily, she confronted George in the front hall, and during a barrage of loud verbal exchange, she let out a chilling scream. From amongst the gardening tools sprawled out on the floor, he had picked up a hammer and hit her hard in the stomach. As with the fire incident, he then calmly sat down again in his chair and continued to read his paper without an ounce of remorse. I felt extremely guilty and very sorry for Philomena because, although we were not particularly close, she had on this occasion, defended me against him.

A number of years prior to these incidents, he had served two years in the

Royal Air Force. During the 1950s, young men around the age of 18 years were required by law to join one of the armed forces and serve two years on what was known as National Service. It was hoped that this would mean our country would be prepared should another World War flare up again. However, I am sure there were political and other social reasons for this. I have often wondered if this period in his life had been a bad experience and perhaps that had turned him into a monster. There have been calls today for the reintroduction of National Service, for young women as well as men and although I agree in principal, I have my reservations.

 I think it was after the hammer incident on my sister that my fear of George turned to suppressed hatred. What I could not understand however, was how such an evil man could have found himself such a lovely, caring, good-natured wife and later go on to have children. I often asked God why he allowed this wicked man to have children, while my adored cousin Sheena, the best person in my life at that time, was unable to have children of her own.

My physical and emotional welfare depended upon this family. They were the role models I was to look up to. The feeling of 'not belonging', of being 'different' to them, was to prove to be a psychological protective shield because I would think to myself, 'I cannot be related to these people', I would not treat anyone like this'. Thoughts like these helped to block their

attempts to instil in me their hypocritical morals.

Chapter Three

St. Mary's Primary School

At the bottom of Park Drive stands St. Mary's Roman Catholic Primary School. How I longed to go there! As we were Catholics I knew I would one day, but I was only four years old and you had to be five, or very nearly five to attend. Until then I used to stand on the pavement and watch the boys and girls coming out at the end of the day. How lucky we were to have a school so close by and not have to walk for miles in all kinds of weather twice a day, as generations before us had done.

At last, that wonderful day came when it was my turn to go to school. My schooldays were arguably, the happiest of my life. I had a thirst for knowledge that sadly, I did not recognize until much later in my life. Nevertheless, I entered into every subject with enthusiasm, although this did not help me much, as I only ever obtained average results. The classroom seemed huge to a child like me who was small for her age, but we had access to a quadrangle where there was apple & cherry trees that in springtime offered a magnificent show of blossom. To this day, spring is still my favourite time of year and its beautiful display of blossom always evokes happy memories of my early schooldays. Besides the usual desks and teachers table, there was a sand pit the size of a snooker table, and it seemed to me as high as one. School was a magical place to me and that feeling stayed with me throughout my entire learning years.

The Headmaster at St. Mary's was Mr. Pollock. He was small, balding, and wore glasses. Each time I see Dads Army on television, I cannot help raise a smile as Captain Mainwaring reminds me of him. However, the headmaster and his wife who followed him are the ones I recall more vividly. Their name was Mr. & Mrs. Kirkwood and besides teaching, Mrs. Kirkwood played the organ and conducted the choir at Our Lady & St.Ninian. Mr. Kirkwood left a lasting impression on me not for anything he may have contributed within school hours, but outside school. We were collecting money for the guy, which would enable us to buy fireworks for bonfire night, and knocked on his door. Instead of giving a donation for our fireworks, he lectured us about the true meaning of bonfire night, what it meant to Catholics, and the execution of Guy Fawkes along with his companions, for their failed attempt to blow up the Houses of Parliament and the King. That was the first and last time we asked *him* for a contribution.

Mrs. Flaherty was the first teacher I can remember. A tall, white haired woman who wore glasses and although had an appropriate air of authority on her, also had a warm smile and gentle manner. She presided over the preparations for First Communion and Confirmation ceremonies and taught us the modus operandi of confession. Mrs. Cullen was never my class teacher, but she played piano at assembly or similar occasions and conducted our school choir. I noted the little finger on her right hand was bent, and wondered if that was how one was supposed to play piano. Later, when I began piano lessons I found it was not so because no matter how I tried, I could not get my little finger to bend like that. It was not until some years later I realised she must have had arthritis.

My abiding memories of St. Mary's teachers though are of Mrs. Flynn who taught us in our last year there. She was every bit as nice as any other teacher I had met and I particularly remember her for three things.

Firstly, she used to read us a story in instalments two or three times a week called Wopsy. He was the guardian angel of a little boy in Africa who, no matter what difficulties he got into, looked after him and kept him safe. Although my religion has taught me that we all have a guardian angel, for me the story of Wopsy just strengthened that belief, which I still hold to-day.

It also left me with the lifelong impression that children in Africa needed a guardian angel far more than we did.

Secondly, she would occasionally hold a spelling Bee. I loved these, as I was rather good at spelling. It's a matter of opinion if I still am. The whole class would stand up, she would ask us in turn to spell a word, and if you got it wrong, you had to sit down. The last person left standing would receive 3d in old money, which is probably around one and a halfpence to-day and could be either a single brass coloured coin, 'a thruppenny bit', or three single copper pennies. This was a great deal of money to a child in those days and I am proud to say I won it more than once. On one such occasion I was so excited at winning three pennies that I dropped them as I was running outside the school then, to my horror, watched helpless as all three rolled down into a drain. I was gutted!

Thirdly, although Mrs. Flynn was normally a mild-mannered person, one particular day she was provoked into a rage that occurred just as the school bins were about to be emptied. A boy in our class who had constantly produced bad work, and who had an equally bad attitude, presented to her what must have been an exceptionally poor piece of work. After calmly reading his essay, she suddenly shouted her disapproval in words I cannot recall but can well imagine. Then, with the essay still in her hand, she swung her right arm in the air with the kind of powerful backhand motion that would have brought the crowds at Wimbledon to their feet in rapturous applause. This sent the exercise book flying through an open window and on to the schoolyard, at the exact moment the bin lorry was passing. It was with great relief that I was instructed to retrieve the book from the yard; complete with the tyre marks of the lorry across the offending pages as if to make the point; as it gave me the opportunity to release my suppressed laughter at the whole debacle.

It was whilst in her year that we sat the 11 plus exam. This determined which class or grade you were to be placed in at senior school, which in our case was St. Modan's High School one and a half miles away in St. Ninians. I was happy to find I had achieved 66%, but I was more interested which of my classmates were to be in the same class as me, than with scholarly grades. As I have said, I was only an average student, with Mathematics and Science my worst subjects, whilst English, History, Music and Geography my best, though History and Music became my lifelong favourites.

Every year in the town of Falkirk, a schools music festival was held and primary schools from all over Central Scotland participated. The year that was largely memorable for me was when Mrs. Cullen picked our class to represent St. Marys. We must have looked a very impressive sight in our tartan kilts or skirts, grey trousers for the boys, white blouses/shirts, and tartan ties. The kilt I wore was the Sea Forth tartan and I was very proud of it. We sang the immortal Robert Burns lyrics 'Ye Banks and Braes' along with another song, and came fourth. This was a great achievement considering the huge numbers of schools entered.

Sports Day was one of those occasions that you either loved or loathed. I was quite indifferent to them because although I was a good runner, I was hopeless at things like high jump etc. It was also however, an excuse for putting on our Sunday best, which I loved to do. The only problem was that a pretty dress with petticoat could be a proper hindrance when trying to run fast. Perhaps the dressing up theory was because it was more of a fun day in those days, whereas to-day children and probably parents too, look upon it as a highly competitive event that they or their child must win.

As I lived so close to the school, I never had school dinners. There was no-one in my house all day, either because they were working or, in the case of my brother and sister, were at St. Modan's and did not come home at lunchtime. Instead, I had a home-cooked meal at Isobel's house. When my contemporaries talk about how horrid their school dinner was, I sometimes wish I had eaten some if only to say that I knew what they meant.

Sometimes the school hall would be used for a social evening for the grown-ups. One particular year on 30th November, a St. Andrew's Day dance took place, and as was customary, every family contributed sandwiches, cakes, and liquid refreshments. Before the dance was in full swing, a number of the excess sandwiches etc. were brought to our house. I was given strict instructions not to touch any of it as it was to be distributed amongst the community the next day. However, a plate of salmon sandwiches took my fancy, so thinking they would not be missed amongst the splendid mountain of goodies, I tucked in and thoroughly enjoyed them. Unfortunately, they did not agree with me and I was up all through the night being sick. Furthermore, I did not put another salmon sandwich to my mouth for years. I also had to confess yet another sinful act to Father McAlister at my next confession.

As was the case in most Catholic schools, we would occasionally have a visit from nuns or a priest currently working with the poor in Britain, and third world countries such as Africa. I especially remember Father Tortellano who was a Franciscan monk whose family lived in Bannockburn. On one of his visits home, he brought some holy pictures of various saints to distribute amongst us. I received one of St. Francis of Assisi, who besides being the founder of the Franciscan Order of monks who take care of the poor, was also the patron Saint of animals. In the picture, St. Francis is holding a bird in the palm of his hand whilst other various animals sit around him. As I too loved animals, St. Francis became my favourite saint.

Every year, the teachers would ask us children to collect rose hips to send to the nuns who would make rose-hip syrup that they could sell. Numerous wild rose bushes grew alongside the river track beyond the Thunder Bridge towards Millhall, so most of us would excitedly go off in pairs, carrying a huge doubled handled strong bag, to collect them. One of Isobel's daughters Moira, was a regular companion of mine, and on one of these picking adventures, she and I were making our way back home when out of nowhere a man appeared claiming to know of a tree that had pears growing on it. In order for us to see this tree, we would have to follow him a short distance just off to the left of our track. As we had never known nor even heard of a pear tree growing anywhere in the area, we did the unthinkable and followed him. Although we children knew we should never speak to, or go with strangers, we felt no fear of danger from this man and sure enough, there was the pear tree and the pears! Furthermore, although it was a hot summer day, this man wore a leather flying type jacket and had a leather glove on one hand, which he tucked inside the jacket. After he pointed out the pears, he waved us on our way. We never relayed the encounter to anyone, nor indeed ever discussed it with one another again, probably from fear of a telling off for speaking to him, let alone following him, but it stayed with me throughout my recollections as a very sinister meeting.

Since I loved school, it was rare that I was absent. Unlike some children who would feign an illness to stay off school, I was upset if I became too ill to attend. One such rare occasion, was when I had tonsillitis and had to stay in bed at cousin Isobel's house. Although I was happy to be looked after by her, it was still tortuous to see her children go off to school, whilst I had to stay at home. Overall, however, we were a relatively healthy generation of kids. The arrival of Penicillin a couple of decades earlier, along with inoculations against Diphtheria and Poliomyelitis, meant we stood a better chance of a healthy childhood compared to our parents' generation. Moreover, for us living in surroundings of clean fresh air, our chances of good health increased still further. Daily doses of Cod Liver Oil, spoonfuls of pure Malt, and Syrup of Figs all helped too, and along with many other old-fashioned remedies and preventative medicines, I am happy to see they are re-appearing in many of today's household medicine cabinets.

Schooldays thus far had been an extremely happy time for me. Therefore, when I walked out of St. Mary's gates for the last time, it was with a heavy heart and feelings of apprehension for what lay ahead.

Chapter Four

Community Players

Everyone had a role to play in post-war communities, where each knew their place and all carried out their responsibilities as best they could. In this respect, Bannockburn was just such a place. Husbands like cousin Isobel's went to work Monday and on Friday would hand their pay packet over to their wife, their duty as hunter-gatherer thus fulfilled. Their wives would then assume control of the family purse strings by paying the weekly bills such as rent and coal, money put aside for the electric meter and food shopping, along with any other bill necessary to run a thriving and usually growing household. In our house, aunty Betty would arrange rows of money on the sideboard, each representing a bill to be paid.

Children went to school and the older siblings could leave school Friday and begin work Monday, thus contributing to the upkeep of the home. If a child was particularly bright and the family could manage without their monetary contribution, he would go to University. If a boy or girl, chose to join the armed forces, then not only was their family proud of them, but the whole town was too. It was common practice for the privilege of a University place, to be reserved for the boys in the family. If you were a girl and were considered bright, you might go to a teacher training college, or to a teaching hospital to become a nurse. It was more usual for girls however, to leave school at 15 yrs of age and start work in an office, shop, or factory in order to supplement the household income. This was the case for Philomena, Sheena and later, myself. A few years later, the females would settle down to married life with a home and children of their own, usually not far from their mother's home.

The elderly also had a role to play, by helping the mums to look after the younger pre-school children: The only nurseries that were around then were the ones that grew plants and flowers: They were always at hand with good sound advice too, along with solutions to anything that required one. Along with teachers, the local police officer, priest or minister and doctor, these were the pillars of our society and were all treated with respect by everyone.

Arguably, the late 1950s and early 1960s was the time unmarried pregnancies became more open, although shotgun weddings became more common too. This type of wedding usually meant that the bride was pregnant as she walked down the aisle, to be met by a sometimes-reluctant bridegroom and father-to-be. Women who chose not to marry the father of their unborn child, gained more support from their family than those from a generation before. Bannockburn's residents were no exception, especially when one of my extended cousins fell pregnant, and she chose not to marry the child's father. After the initial shock and consternation, the family rallied around and supported her wholeheartedly. The elderly residents were usually the first to express their hypocritical disgust, albeit behind their own closed doors, but on the birth of the illegitimate child, would produce a hand knitted garment or present for the baby. Therefore, what had begun as a scandal nine months previously, became a happy event for all and the new baby 'sister' or 'brother' joined the growing establishment.

Although Bannockburn of the 1950s possessed physical charm and beauty, as a community it was just like many others of the time. Civil liberties meant we children had freedom to play in and explore our surroundings in complete and utter safety without infringing on anyone else's person nor property. Except that is, for the odd scrumping for apples, which is a compulsory activity for any generation. Race issues meant who could run the fastest and the worst thing you could catch from the opposite sex was boy or girl germs! We were never in fear for our lives from mugging, gangs, drugs, shootings, or knife attacks. The things we feared most were our parents wrath if we had behaved badly, the local Policeman and perhaps, for some of us anyway, the parish priest: Or rather the fear of hells-fire and damnation if we had behaved *very* badly: We all knew our local police officer's name, but more to the point, he knew ours.

PC Hulme lived on the next street after Park Crescent called Firs Crescent, so even if he was off duty, he could take a naughty child by the scruff of the neck, march it to it's parent's door and then be back home in the blink of an eye. This might include a cuff around the ear from him for good measure, but it would most definitely not include a suit for compensation from the parents. On the contrary, it usually resulted in a cuff around the other ear from the parents because the child was naughty in the first place. Another aspect of such a situation was the shame parents would feel that a police officer had brought their child home for behaving badly. For a number of years throughout the 1950s, the officers at Bannockburn police station continued to sound the air raid alarm, and more than once, I was unfortunate to be passing at the time! I suspect it went off more often *after* the war than during.

Our local doctor Dr. King lived on the same premises as his surgery on the Bannockburn Road, halfway up the hill towards the top of the town. If his doorbell rang due to a minor emergency, he would think nothing of attending to it. One day I was one of those emergencies. On my way home from school I saw cousin Isobel who told me to go into her house to wash my hands and face, as I would be going into Stirling for some new shoes from the shop where Sheena worked. I was so excited as I ran towards her door, that I did not notice a twig laying on the ground and consequently tripped over it. My forehead hit the metal threshold, which sent blood from a split left eyebrow pouring down my face, and my subsequent spine chilling screams, could be heard 500yds (around 160 meters.) away. This brought Isobel running in and when she saw me, immediately grabbed the dishcloth from the kitchen sink and slapped it on my eye. She then took me to Dr. King's, running all the way. Some children were still coming out of school and as we passed they asked what had happened. Even through the excruciating pain, I thought she was so funny when she replied, "She tripped o'er a haystack and a hen kicked hur"! I had guessed it was a bad cut because usually when any of us had a scratch or similar on our faces, she would pick up the corner of her paisley patterned apron, and wipe it off. Those aprons seemed to have a thousand uses, from wiping dirty faces to carrying anything the wearer, when gathered up; (usually Grannies and Mammies) asked it to. Therefore, when in this situation the wet dishcloth was required, I knew it must be serious.

As I said earlier, despite it being outside surgery hours, Dr. King took me in to have it seen to. He said "Now I'm going to clean it with disinfectant so keep your eyes closed". However, although I kept the wounded eye closed I couldn't help opening the other so I could take a peep at what he was doing. Consequently, the disinfectant ran into my good eye. "Oh my god!" I cried inwardly, "now I'll go blind"! The burning sensation was excruciating. He then put a few stitches in with the skill of a ship's surgeon during the Battle of Trafalgar, then with much the same decorum, tossed me back into harsh reality. I still carry the battle scar from that surgeon's needlework to this day, but also gratitude for having saved my sight! As for the new shoes, when Sheena heard what had happened, she brought me the loveliest pair of red shoes I had ever seen, or half-seen!

Apart from these respected figures of authority, every town or village had its own characters and Park Crescent was no exception. Black Joe was the local tramp who lived in and slept on, the park benches. Black Joe was not his real name however, it was just a nickname given to him by the town's children because he had black hair and a very black beard. His real name was Willie McEwan and the older townsfolk would say "Aye Willie" as they passed him, to which he always responded "Aye so-and-so". He was often seen standing by a side entrance to the park, smoking a discarded cigarette butt he had picked up. To an outsider he probably looked frightful, but we were not afraid of him, as he never bothered us except to say 'hello'. He had two spinster sisters who lived nearby but did not, or would not, live with them. It was as though he was rebelling against society and decided to remove himself from it. I have often wondered if he had been in a war and his way of life was a consequence of his experiences in that war. It was common throughout the 1950's, to come across someone whose experience of war had left them unable to cope with post-war life. I suspect many towns had a man like Joe. I remember him fondly and pray he found peace.

Someone I *was* rather nervous of however was a youth named Hawkeye. He was around ten years older than me and lived near us with his parents and sister and they had a beautiful but fierce, Alsatian dog called Prince. It is debatable which one I was more nervous of, the dog or Hawkeye. I do not know why everyone called him Hawkeye, but I have a couple of theories of my own, which I will not record here. He was a typical 1950s Teddy boy, with the DA hairstyle, (which stood for duck's arse, so called because it was swept back at the sides and met in the middle at the back), thick crepe soled suede shoes, commonly known as brothel creepers, vividly coloured socks, and three quarter length jackets with velvet collars and drainpipe trousers. Sometimes they wore shirts with these that had frills down the front. Teddy boys had a reputation for being menacing, intimidating, and hung around in gangs of around five, six, or more. If I was walking along the street and came across Hawkeye and his friends, I would step onto the road to avoid passing between them. My fears were of course groundless because they never bothered me and Hawkeye was in fact, always quite pleasant towards me. Unfortunately, they had acquired a fearsome reputation that, in my revised opinion, was quite unfounded. I met up with him many years later on a visit to Bannockburn, and he was overjoyed at seeing me again and I was happy to see him too.

Hawkeye's mum too was an easily recognizable figure in the community. Her name was Peggy, and she was a cleaner on the Alexander buses at Stirling and then Bannockburn bus depot. Her job meant she worked night shift so would come home in the morning, when most people were setting off to work or school. I often used to see her in blue cotton dungarees, her hair in rollers wrapped up in a turban headscarf, holding a cigarette in her hand or dangling it from the corner of her mouth, coming home after making those blue buses sparkle.

Again as with many communities, we had among us one or two people who had what would be termed today as learning difficulties. I would not for one moment wish to belittle them by naming them here therefore, suffice it to say they were lovely, gentle, mild mannered individuals whom Park

Crescent took to their hearts and would challenge anyone who caused them offence or harm. Thankfully, there were no prejudices towards anyone who was different in any way. On the contrary, we all looked after them and treated them just like anybody else.

I fondly remember one individual who was the archetypal gentle giant. He lived near me with his mother and had lovely rosy red cheeks and blonde curly hair. He had the loveliest smile and always passed the time of day with me if I bumped into him. He could always be seen in blue overalls and although he was huge next to me, I always felt safe and happy to be around him.

Another of our neighbours worked for a Scottish Laird on his highland estate and part of his job included looking after the laird's birds of prey. He would often bring them home and keep them in a huge hut in his garden, but sometimes they could be seen in the house perched on dining chairs at intervals around the living room. They would include eagle hawks, falcons, and the occasional owl. When I called at their house for the children to come out to play, I always refused the offer to come inside because the birds looked so fierce and frightening to a little girl. On the rare occasion when the Laird visited, he made a grand impressive sight walking down our street, wearing his full highland dress with his long pure white hair and beard. This was an unusual sight in the central lowlands of Scotland, so everyone would strain their necks to have a look. Later however, when the family moved home to the Laird's estate, the house was fumigated before another family could move in.

One character that was a less impressive sight however, was a neighbour who could be found sitting with her window as high up as it could go, with her huge breasts hanging out over the sill. This huge fat woman could be seen there anytime of day or evening, watching the comings and goings of everyone else on the street, wearing such a dour expression on her face that you had to pluck up courage just to say good morning! Her voice was as loud as a foghorn and when she called her children in for tea, she could be heard by all of us, even if we were not in the immediate vicinity. If only she had been in the crow's nest of the Titanic in 1912, they might not have crashed into the iceberg, because she could have bellowed the alarm, which would have been heard all the way back in Southampton. On a trip back to Bannockburn many years later, I found that same woman still sitting by that same window, looking exactly as she did all those years ago, still wearing that same dour look on her face.

Park Crescent also had characters who were involved in the day-to-day running of the lives of the community. Besides a number of small grocers such as Henderson's then Gowans, there was only one large food store that served the Bannockburn community in the 1950s and 60's. It was the Co-operative Wholesale Society, or the Co-op for short. Although it sold most items on the housewives' shopping list, communities like Park Crescent also relied on individual traders who provided a mobile service.

Bunty Reynolds was the woman who drove the co-op bread van. She always had a splendid array of bread and cakes on her huge shelves in the van. Hail, rain or snow, Bunty could be relied upon to do her round and was always a pleasant welcome sight, especially for the elderly, or those who could not get to the shops. Willie Agnew had a fruit and vegetable cart that was drawn by a huge grey horse and he too could always be relied upon to turn up in all kinds of weather, sometimes two or three times a week. We children would often ask him if he had any rotten fruit to which he would respond by handing us an over-ripe banana, bruised apple, or a squashed tomato. He later progressed to a van and consequently, Park Crescent's gardens did not bloom quite as beautiful.

Mr. Miller, along with his wife and later their son, owned and worked the farm next to St. Mary's primary school. They had a daughter too who attended a private school in Dunblane, but who never came to play with us. However, I do not recall if we even asked her. Perhaps even at such a young age, we unknowingly felt the class divide between private and state education. Families either had their milk delivered by Mr. Miller or from the local co-op. If anyone required extra milk, they could go down to the farm anytime day or night, regardless whether or not they were a regular customer of his. Mrs. Miller would use a long handled dipping ladle to draw the milk direct from the churn and pour it into the bottle. She then placed a foil top over the neck and with a little machine press, sealed the top onto the bottle. I remember quite vividly the smell from the dairy, especially if the bottles had just been washed in boiling water. You could have eaten your dinner off the floor, as it smelled so clean and fresh. Although there were laws regarding the sale of milk from the churn, such as cooling and filtering of milk, farmers did not have Health and Safety Executive officers breathing down their neck as they have today. Furthermore, I do not recall anyone from our community falling ill because of drinking milk direct from the churn.

There was only one thing about going down to the farm which scared me a little, and that was Mrs. Miller's geese and ducks. If they were freely roaming around, they would charge at you like scrap yard guard dogs. In fact, they probably made better guard dogs. On more than one occasion, they had me pinned with my back against the dairy wall, where I would stand rigid with fear until Mrs. Miller came and moved them away.

Mr. Gray owned the bakery near Dr. King's surgery but a little way back from the main road. Besides beautiful cakes and pastries, he baked the most gorgeous rolls (bread cakes) and delivered them door to door. Whenever I visit Bannockburn, I make a point of buying half a dozen or so rolls, which always reminds me of the heavenly aroma coming from Mr. Gray's bakery. Although he lived with his family in the council houses opposite St. Mary's on Park Drive, his daughter, like that of Mr. and Mrs Miller, attended a private school.

Every Friday the fish man came round in his little van with a good variety of fresh fish. It was a common ritual amongst catholic families not to eat meat on Fridays. I believe this had something to do with the day of the week Christ died for us. Therefore fish was the preferred, and perhaps the only, alternative. Many non-catholic families however, also followed this ritual and so it became traditional that most people had fish for tea every Friday. On a rare occasion, a fish & chip van came around, usually in the evening. We could smell him before we saw him and it was utter heaven to our senses. However, some parents were reluctant to allow their children to buy chips from him in case it gave the impression that they had not fed them at teatime. It was quite acceptable though, for the whole family to indulge in a fish supper.

The ragman's van was another happy sight for us children. He would ring a loud bell calling out "any old rags" to which the children responded by running to their mums asking for old woollen jumpers or anything else with holes in, so they could be exchanged for balloons or another small toy or similar item. By far the favourite van to come around our street though was the ice-cream van. Nowhere else in the United Kingdom, or maybe even the planet, could there be found ice-cream vans like the ones we had in Scotland in the 1950s and probably still do to-day. Not only did they sell the obligatory cold white stuff, in plain and chocolate wafers and cones along with iced lollies, but you could buy different flavoured pop, sweets, chocolate, biscuits, and cigarettes too. You could even buy an aspirin from the ice-cream van and if a smoker was strapped for cash, they could buy single cigarettes rather than a whole packet. My aunty Betty's favourite was a walnut whip, but she could never pronounce it right and would call it a whipped cream walnut. Many were the times she would send me out to fetch one for her without, not surprisingly, asking if I would like anything.

Every couple of months or so a salesperson came to our house driving a small green van and carrying a brown leather suitcase. He was a tall thin man of Asian/Indian origin and always looked immaculate in his suit and trilby hat. We children never knew his surname, so we called him John the darkie, much to the adults' horror and dismay, for which we were soundly scolded. He was a lovely warm friendly person, who always had a smile for us. He would place his suitcase on the living room floor and when he opened it, there was a lovely collection of woman's clothes. Every single item was neatly presented in a clear shiny polythene bag, which made a rustling noise as John spread them out to be viewed. My aunt often bought something, either nylons or a petticoat and one day she bought me my very first pair of trousers from him. She of course chose the brown nylon stretch slacks with yellow stripes. I must have looked like a bumblebee but I did not care, because they had stirrups under the foot, which were fashionable at the time and I did not own any fashionable items of clothing. I only had them a couple of months though because unknown to me, someone had painted the kitchen chairs and when I rose up, the yellow stripes were accompanied by white stripes, but only on the bum! Aunty betty never liked those fashionable slacks in the first place so needless to say, she never bought me a pair again. John's parents had known my grandparents during the war, and they used to bring fresh eggs and other produce to our house, which were hard to acquire during those difficult years. Therefore, my aunt, through buying something from John from time to time, was probably repaying their kindness. I sincerely hope life was good to John.

These trades' people and characters all played a huge part in our daily life and I am sure the services they provided, along with their friendly chatter and gossip, is sadly missed by those who are old enough to remember them.

Street Party,Park Gardens, Bannockburn

Chapter Five

We Never Had it So Good

Thankfully, we were not as deprived as our older siblings had been during the war years, especially where sweets were concerned. It is widely believed that sweets did not become available again, or 'off the rations' until around 1952. Who could possibly forget Bazooka Joe pink bubbly gum? Our jaws would ache as we tried to chew our way through one of those. There was not one child who did not get into trouble with their mother for blowing such a huge bubble that covered their entire face and then stuck to their hair when it burst. Mojos, fruit salads, black jacks, gob stoppers, penny caramels, to name just a few, were very popular. It was a wonder our second teeth came through at all after getting our baby teeth wrapped around those!! My own particular favourites were rainbow drops and chocolate drops.

One day whilst out walking with Philomena and her friends, she sent me into the sweet shop for a quarter of chocolate drops, (about 100grms) but by the time I caught up with them, she declared, "There's never a quarter here!" "Och aye thur is", I replied. Of course, she was right. I had eaten some whilst deliberately dragging my heels behind them. Father Mac, here I come!

'The Rations' was a term that even in the late 1950s was still used when meaning the food shopping. I can recall the adults in our house saying "I'm just going up for the rations", when referring to food shopping. Later, the term used in Bannockburn for the food shopping was 'the messages'. As was the norm everywhere in the country during the war years, in the 1950's mums knew how to make the most of every scrap of food and nothing was wasted.

Some like cousin Isobel and Jock grew their own vegetables. I recall one winter day being told to fetch a leek from their garden using a kitchen fork, but the ground was so hard with frost, the fork handle snapped. Clothes were handed down to younger siblings, and some items would have hems dropped to a fraction of an inch to last as long as possible. Fashion was not as important in some households as in others. Toys too were passed on for as long as they were serviceable. When the ragman came around, we could only take items of clothing out to him if there was absolutely no life left in the garment at all.

A famous politician is recorded saying that at this period in our country's history, that is the 1950s, we had 'never had it so good'. Perhaps we children of the 1950s did have it good; it was certainly a better life than those in the

1940s and before; only a decade had passed since they had endured depravations of the material kind and losses of the human kind that thankfully, we could not comprehend. Nevertheless, some cupboards held more skeletons than food, where secrets and lies were stored but never discussed. Pre-marital, extra-marital, and post divorce affairs were all kept quiet, even those that produced offspring. Children were seen and not heard, and their opinion was neither asked nor given. I can still hear the instruction "Speak when you are spoken to" ringing in my ears. We could not leave the table after a meal without saying "Please may I leave the table?" Moreover, we definitely did *not* get any pudding if we had not eaten the main course! Children called their parents mum and dad, unlike some household's to-day where children are treated as 'mini adults' and are allowed to call their parents by their Christian names. I would never dream of calling my elders be they relative or neighbour, by their Christian name. Even as a grown-up with children of my own, I find it difficult to call older neighbours by their Christian name, even when they insist on it.

People would often go out during the day and leave their doors unlocked because no-one would dream of breaking in to steal anything or cause anyone harm. Everyone was more or less in the same financial bracket and they all possessed much the same as each other, so there was never a motive to steal from neighbours. If any child was caught getting up to no good by an adult other than a member of their own family, they could still expect to get the customary clip round the ear then sent on their way. This was the BT era, Before Television, when children were still able and sometimes more than willing, to provide their own entertainment. Skipping ropes, peevers (or hopscotch in England) kick the can, hide and seek, marbles, along with the more traditional games such as cricket, football and rounders, kept us all occupied and happy for hours on end. We did not always have to go to the park to play, as we were very lucky to have a grassy area near our homes, which served very well as a football, cricket or rounders pitch. I particularly loved football and if I had been born a boy, I have often wondered if I would have made it my career. Not that being a girl stopped me playing. Even when I was of working age, I would come home from work and relish a game of kick-about with the boys from next door.

During one of these games, a friend of theirs came over and asked if he could join in, but was told no. He responded by saying "but SHE'S playing", to which the boys replied "Aye, but she's better than you!" I felt honoured by the compliment. Of course, there was also the seasonal fun and games like conkers in the autumn and sledging in winter.

Bannockburn in the 1950s had its very own cinema called The Regent. It was owned at the time by a man called Joe Mooney and was situated at the top of Bannockburn town on the corner of The Fues and Quakerfield. The Saturday afternoon matinees were very popular when Flash Gordon, Tarzan, Roy Rodgers and Trigger, transported us into a magical world of adventure, danger and excitement. Of course, that was when the older Teddy Boys and girls upstairs gave us some respite from throwing their unfinished ice creams and cigarette ends over the balcony on to us below. It was a wonder we could see the screen at all due to the thick haze of cigarette smoke that floated across the length and breadth of the cinema. The sweet kiosk was located in the right hand corner of the foyer, and there we could buy our 'ammunition'. This usually consisted of aniseed balls or similar, that we could throw at the 'enemy'! I particularly enjoyed a packet of crisps with its own little blue bag of salt. Not so enjoyable however, when chewed on by mistake in the darkness.

Furthermore, Saturday afternoon matinees were always noisy events, especially when the good guys beat the bad guys and the place erupted in ear piercing cheering. Nevertheless, it was an institution missed by many after it was closed then pulled down and replaced by shops.

A couple, who lived around the corner from us and did not have children of their own, bought one of the first television sets to arrive in our neighbourhood. They allowed us children to come and watch it for a small charge, around a ha'penny I think (about halfpence today). After school or on Saturday mornings we stood in an orderly queue outside their front door, each of us clutching our precious entrance fee in our hand, excitedly waiting in anticipation, to watch Children's Hour or The Cisco Kid. Later, another neighbour who had acquired a Television, allowed us to watch free of charge and on arrival, we took off our shoes and left them in a corner of her kitchen. When it was time to go home, it took us a while to rummage through the mountain of shoes to find our own, because most of us wore the same kind.

The Cisco Kid and his sidekick Pancho was a popular cowboy programme and is the earliest I can remember. Muffin the Mule, Watch with Mother; which included Picture Book on Monday, Andy Pandy Tuesday, Bill and Ben Wednesday, Rag Tag and Bobtail Thursday and the Woodentops Friday; all came under the umbrella of the aforementioned Children's Hour. Champion the Wonder Horse, The Lone Ranger, William Tell, Robin Hood, Circus Boy, and my own favourite Lassie all followed later. By now, most households had their own television set, and whilst we relished in other children's programmes such as Crackerjack and Pinky and Perky, the adults were enjoying the likes of Dixon of Dock Green, Armchair Theatre, Hancock's half hour, and more especially in Scotland, The White Heather

Club.

It was thanks to Lassie though, that I learned to ride a bike. Philomena, along with Isobel's daughter Sheila, were teaching me to ride one day and I hated every minute of it. As it was nearly time for Lassie to come on T.V. I cried out "I dinnae want tae ride a bike I want tae go in and see Lassie" They said I was not going in to see Lassie until I could ride it. That day, I learned to ride the bike!

Even though television was welcomed by all age groups, it did not rule our lives as it seems to do to-day. Apart from the aforementioned games and bike-riding along with roller skating, we girls would collect and exchange scraps. These were made of thin paper and were colourful pictures which we could buy in the shops for a few pennies and usually came in strips or a packet. We each would choose an old book from home; usually a hard backed one, and place an individual scrap in each page of the book. These pictures would be of cherubs on clouds, flowers in baskets, animals and angels besides other things. They often came in various sizes and if you had a full set, they would make a good bargaining tool for exchanging with friends. You could of course exchange single or double sizes, that way you could build up a good collection. You were the envy of everyone if you had a full book which included lots of full sets. This was a particularly good fun way of spending a few hours, especially on a rainy day.

Another rainy day activity was to cut out paper dolls from the back of our girl comics such as Bunty. This comic was quite popular because of the different clothes for Bunty's wardrobe which were featured each week. Some of the stories were good too, such as The Four Marys and Tootsie. Nora and Tilly were also cutout dolls from a comic or magazine that we loved to dress up each week in different outfits. The forerunners of Cindy and Barbie perhaps?

Apart from these few occasions when the boys played their own games and the girls theirs, we mostly all played or hung around together. We were fiercely loyal towards anyone from our 'scheme' or territory and especially united in an "all for one, one for all" call when confronted by outsiders. Bonfire night was one of those times when confrontations were inevitable, especially in the days leading up to it. Our bonfire took place in a huge crater-like area at the top of Park Drive where the first four or so houses on the right now stand. It would be built up gradually over a few days so we had to be on full alert from thieves, especially from the Hillparkies, as we called the children from Hillpark. They were notorious for stealing wood and other items from our pile and would often blame us if any of theirs disappeared. I cannot think why! As the open space where our bonfire was situated could be seen from my house, I had the best opportunity of keeping a lookout for any would-be thief so I could raise the alarm quite quickly and scare them off. Sometimes though, there would be much grappling over contested, conquered loot, and I don't think either bonfire was ever lit using the original material that it had been built with in the first place. The mums of Park Crescent always made sure no child went without a hot treat. Whilst holding a sparkler, some chestnuts and potatoes were pushed into the burning embers on the bottom periphiry of the fire and, when cooked, teased out with a stick. Health and Safety was also provided by the aforementioned mums. Fireworks were few but usually set off around the fire and everyone always had a good time.

Dookin' fur apples was great fun too. A bowl of water containing a number of apples along with a selection of nuts was placed on the kitchen floor. Each child took a turn to kneel on a chair with the handle of a fork in our mouth, hands behind our back, and let the fork drop into the bowl to pierce an apple. When every child had 'won' an apple, we then took it in turn to get down on our knees, again with our hands behind our back, and gather up as many nuts as we could using only our mouths. The poor mums' floors were always flooded with water, but many happy, exhausted children did not need coaxing to bed *that* night.

Another event that gave us kids a thrill, took place on the day of a wedding. When the bride left her house to go to the church, it was traditional to have a 'scramble' (pronounced scrammel!). The father of the bride threw a handful of coins from the window of the wedding car as it set off, and children would scramble to pick up what they could. Sometimes though, from amoungst the mums who had come to see the bride, an outstretched Paisley patterned apron could be seen trying to catch the coins for their own offspring.

The Regent, Bannockburn

Christmas provided us with precious new toys and books. The Broons or Oor Wullie Annuals were very popular, even compulsory. For the benefit of those who did not read The Sunday Post, they are comedy characters featured on a weekly basis in that paper in Scotland. New bicycles were the reserve of the few well off children. If one appeared in a family, as was the case in ours, it was shared by many, then handed down to younger siblings. We did not usually buy one another presents particularly in our family, as there were too many. However, one year I managed to scrape up enough money (probably from Patrick) to buy Isobel's children a small gift. The older ones did not miss out, as I bought two or three McCowan's toffee selection boxes for the boys and rain-mates for the girls. I wrapped two items of toffees together into individual tiny parcels. The rain-mates were equally tiny as they folded up concertina style into the size of a human thumb. When unfolded, they were plastic transparent hats with drawstring that tied under the chin. Some women found them useful in emergencies, but the younger generation looked upon them as unfashionable. It gave me an enormous amount of pleasure to take my little parcels down to Isobel's house that Christmas Eve.

The adults did their best to make sure Santa Claus brought us something to put a smile on our faces. Sometimes there were new roller skates, bride dolls, sewing machines that actually sewed real stitches, or china tea set. The boys would be delighted with a new cricket bat, real leather 'team ball' (football), or a chemical set. Without exception, everyone who had put up a stocking by the fireplace found in it, an orange, sixpenny bit coin, (two and a half pence to-day) and some sweets. The smell of oranges still reminds me of Christmas today. After Mass or church on Christmas morning, the children of Park Crescent went round to friends or family's homes to show them what Santa Claus had brought.

Chapter Six

Extra Curricular Activities

When I was around nine years old, Aunty Betty informed me that I was to begin piano lessons. A man who lived in Firs Crescent was to teach me one evening per week at a cost of half a crown, or 2/6d. The equivalent today would be 25pence. As we had a piano in the house, practicing would not be a problem. I was not asked if I would like to have piano lessons, but because Sheena, Patrick, and Philomena had all learned to play, it was expected that I would do likewise. They had all however, been taught by a man who lived in Stirling, but when it came to my turn, he had retired so this local man agreed to teach me. He was married and both he and his wife were always very pleasant towards me. However, I always felt rather uncomfortable when he leaned over me from behind to play a piece of music, in order to demonstrate how it should be played, as I could feel his breathe on my neck.

Whenever aunt Betty had visitors, she would send me upstairs to the sitting room to play piano for them. I did not mind this in principle because I liked playing piano and I could quite easily get lost in a lovely, dreamy melody. What did bother me though was the freezing cold temperature of the room itself. It would sometimes be so cold in there I could see my own breathe. Although there was an electric fire, I was forbidden to switch it on. It was a coal effect fire, with two electric bars positioned above a plastic imitation of hot coals, which looked real because of the red light bulb situated underneath. There was a separate switch for each bar, but attempting to turn them on without my aunt's knowledge was futile, because they made such a loud tin 'clunk' sound that she could hear it from downstairs; to which she would bellow from below "You can switch that fire off, it costs money for the electric"! This was the case on ordinary practice evenings, but if visitors were present and I asked her permission to put the fire on, she would allow it.

Ballet lessons were also on our out-of-school-activities list. On Saturday mornings Philomena, Moira and I, would take the three-mile bus ride to Stirling, to a hall down The Craigs that was used by a number of organisations, including the Boys Brigade. We used the hall first, which meant that those boys who had arrived early, would peek in at us doing our ballet routine and have a good giggle, accompanied by remarks such as "Oh that reminds me, my mammy wants her chimney sweepin'", referring to our tutus or, "Where's the rest o' yer froak, did ye furget tae bring it?"

Miss McLaughlan was our teacher and we all loved her. She was qualified to teach up to a high standard, the next stage being The Royal Ballet School in Glasgow. Philomena was an excellent tap and ballet dancer who could have gone on to Glasgow, but this would have been too expensive so the opportunity passed her by. I do not know who was the most disappointed she, or Miss McLaughlan.

Ballet displays were wonderful events when we could invite our family and friends to come and see what we had accomplished. For one of these occasions, our class did a dance routine to the tune 'The Irish Washer-Women'. Besides our beautiful white tutus, we wore emerald green satin headscarves and aprons, and part of the routine meant we had to untie our aprons and place them in our washing baskets. However, during rehearsals, my apron acquired a knot which refused to become undone. One of my classmates had to rescue me from the situation by untying the rogue apron for me. Therefore, it was with great relief that on the night, my rogue apron behaved itself. My sister's class did a Russian tap dance routine and they all looked beautiful in their lilac satin fur trimmed ballet tutus and Cossack style hats to match. At the same time as we were attending ballet classes, a couple of Isobel's other children had elocution lessons and, along with

Philomena performed in locally produced plays.

Another after school activity was a youth club held at St. Mary's every Thursday evening. A married couple, whose names I cannot remember so I will call them Mr. and Mrs. McKenzie, offered us activities they hoped would interest us. When Mr. McKenzie formed a choir and the opportunity arose to appear at a concert in Falkirk, my aunt refused to give permission for me to attend. The reason for this was that we were expected to wear a small amount of make-up and she was totally against the idea. When one or two others could not attend either, our choir was withdrawn.

One evening the McKenzies brought a bundle of scripts for a play they had hoped we would be interested in performing. It was called 'The Shilling – a – Week Man' and was about the man who called weekly on the homes of poor families who had borrowed money from him, or his organisation, collecting re-payments. I found this particularly great fun, but sadly there was not enough interest from my peers to continue with it. Mrs. McKenzie's enthusiasm was not doused by this though, and she announced that she was willing to take us to the swimming baths and to teach those of us who could not swim. There was a good uptake of this offer and we were all excited the following week, as we arrived at the Riverside School baths in Stirling.

I did not tell Mrs. McKenzie however, that since my sister and her friends had pushed me into the deep end of the paddling pool in the park when I was around four or five years old, it left me terrified of water. Moreover, I had not told anyone, not even my family and friends. I was nonetheless, very keen to learn to swim and thought that this would be an opportunity to conquer my fear. Everything seemed to be going along swimmingly, if you'll pardon the pun, despite slipping on the bottom step climbing in to the pool. Until that is, Mrs. McKenzie asked us to form a circle around her so she could speak to us. As we waded towards her I slipped again and lost my footing. Utter panic and terror caused me to splash wildly and, if it hadn't been for one of my friends grabbing hold of me, I was convinced I would have drowned. That was the last straw and to this day I still cannot swim.

The youth club folded soon after as sadly the numbers dwindled, which meant it was not viable to have the school opened up in the evening. I felt extremely sorry for this lovely couple, who were willing to give their time and energy so that we could enjoy some worthwhile interests and activities. Our P.E. Teacher at St. Modan's Miss Mitchell, taught us Scottish Country Dancing, for the small fee of one penny, once a week out of school hours. I adored dancing the jigs and reels such as The Dashing White Sergeant, The Eightsome Reel, and The Gay Gordon, especially at parties or gatherings.

A couple of years later I joined the church choir as one of only three young members. This did not bother me, as I loved singing, and as I could sing Soprano and could harmonise well, I was a welcome addition. Isobel was also a good singer so she too joined, though I now wonder how she ever managed to find the time for rehearsals. These sometimes took place in Mrs. Kirkwood's house which, for Isobel and I was only a short walk down the road. Ice-skating was emerging as a popular pastime and hobby and although Stirling did not have an ice-rink, there was one in Falkirk about a half hour bus ride away. Only one or two of the children in our community took up ice-skating though, whilst a small number joined the Lifebuoys, Boys Brigade, Sea Cadets, Cubs, Boy Scouts, Brownies, or Girl Guides. The children of working class families however, may have enjoyed one of these activities, but it was rare for a child to part-take in two or more at any one time because of the expense involved.

Chapter Seven

Grand Days Out

The summers of the 1950s always seemed to be long, hot, and always sunny. Sometimes it was so hot, that even if we wanted to run around in bare feet we could not, otherwise they were burned by the melting tarmac. The school summer holidays gave us eight fantastic weeks, not only to explore our beautiful local surroundings, but the opportunity to travel further afield too. In the 1950s, foreign holidays had not yet become the norm for the working classes of Bannockburn, but Scotland had many beautiful seaside towns within relatively easy reach for a great day out.

Burntisland and Portobello, on the southern side of the Firth of Forth near Edinburgh, were very popular with families, whilst Kinghorn, St. Andrews and the silver sands at Aberdour, were equally great places to visit on the northern coast of the Firth. I spent many happy days out at these places with cousin Isobel and her children. They were especially great as part of a trip organized by Alexander buses, whose offices aunty Betty and later

Philomena worked in, and for a time Isobel. On these occasions, competitive events like sports day races took place and I particularly remember the one where Isobel won the mothers race. She flew like a bat out of hell and beat all the other mothers by a mile. She was brilliant and I was very proud of her. Also on the trip was an elderly neighbour Mrs. Thompson, whose daughter also worked in the offices and who lived in Park Gardens. Before we set off and whilst everyone was finding their seat on the coach, it became apparent that these seats would not be wide enough to accommodate Mrs. T. Besides being elderly, she was also rather big and everyone was determined that, under no circumstances were we leaving her behind. After some scratching of heads, someone piped up "Go and get my wooden stool from the kitchen, she can sit on that". So the blue painted wooden stool was duly fetched, placed in the aisle of the coach, and with a soft plumped up cushion for comfort, Mrs. T. was able to join everyone else. Thankfully, there was no such thing as Health and Safety then nor rules about seat belts, not that one would have fitted round her anyway! On our return, Mrs. T. remarked that it had been a grand day out and thanked everyone for taking her along.

One particular year, we spent a whole week in a caravan, a bit further afield in Arbroath, south of Dundee on the east coast of Scotland. This was exciting as it had been the farthest any of us children had ever travelled and, as we went by train, it might well have been hundreds of miles away. The holiday party consisted of around 10 or 12 of our family, and as we could not find two caravans in Arbroath to accommodate all of us, a second one was booked at a campsite in Carnoustie, a few short miles down the road. This was great for us as it meant we could visit two places instead of just one, but it must have been a nightmare for the adults. My abiding memory of that holiday though, took place on the day we left to come home. It was a very stormy day and the waves from the North Sea came crashing over the road which led to the railway station. One particularly huge wave thundered over the sea wall defences and crashed down on our coach with such force, that it was nothing short of a miracle that we were not swept out to sea.

Local outings too, were every bit as enjoyable. Half an hour or so by bus took us north through Stirling to Dunblane, where we could play in the shallow waters of the river Allan flowing through the Laigh Hills (pronounced locally as the lay-kills!). This gave us the opportunity to meet and play with children from other communities in the region, which made a nice change. Another local outing, which became one of my favourites, was the walk to the next village of Cowie along with Isobel and Jock and the children, to visit Jock's parents. This usually took place on a Sunday afternoon, when we would already be dressed in our Sunday best for Mass that morning. They were a lovely old couple and I am particularly grateful that they treated me as one of their own, even though they were not my grandparents. As my cousins' granddad had been a miner at the Cowie coal pit, they lived in a house which was part of what was known as the Miner's Rows. (pronounced raws). We spent many happy hours playing on the 'Cowie Bing' (an old slagheap that had been re-claimed by nature and was now grown over with flowering bushes etc.) Later, they were allocated a house on the new housing estate, but my memories remain playing around the open spaced yards of the 'raws', with washing lines all hung out ready for the Monday wash day and then back to granny's for a 'piece 'n jam' from a pan loaf. That is, a slice of bread, butter and jam, from a sliced loaf with lighter coloured and softer crusts than an ordinary plain loaf of bread.

The walk to and from Cowie, particularly on a hot summer day was a lovely experience. It was a typical country walk with roadside bushes displaying an abundance of wild flowers such as white and pink ballerina roses, or the white and yellow flower of the bramble bushes, wild bluebells, grape hyacinths, and many more whose names I cannot remember. It was a safe journey too as there was hardly a vehicle on the road, except perhaps for the Cowie to Dunblane bus which ran about every half hour or so.

Every summer Bannockburn held a Gala Day for the children of the town. It was a very well attended event and seemed as if the whole population of the town was there. Local tradesmen loaned their open top vehicles, some motorised, and others horse drawn, so we children could sit on them, excitedly waving our Union Jack, Saltire, (St. Andrew's Cross), and Scottish Lion Rampant flags. The parade of vehicles, with numbers of children walking behind, usually set off from a designated area, wound through the town, then ended at the bottom park. I can just see the wringing of hands and the tearing out of hair by today's Health & Safety Executives! On disembarking at the huge grassy expanse, each child was given a paper bag inside which were sandwiches, a cake or bun, sweets and a bottle of fizzy pop. After an enjoyable picnic, we played games, held races and other fun filled activities. All things considered, the post-war adults made sure we children of the 1950s had many fun filled days full of happy memories.

A visit to aunty Sadie's house in Stirling was also a pleasant day out. She lived an area of the town called the Cornton in a pre-fabricated house (fondly remembered as a pre-fab.) These were bungalows designed and built in ready-made sections, and offered a quick solution to the housing shortage immediately after the war. They were only supposed to be temporary, but they were still in use nation-wide many years later than originally intended and almost all the residents were reluctant to leave. I sometimes spent the night at aunty Sadie and uncle Fergus's house and, as it was situated near to the railway line, loved it when the whole house shook whenever a train passed by. Although uncle Fergus was unused to having children around, he was kind to us. He was a tall man and, as he came from a Scottish Island, spoke with a beautiful accent. He had a very good job as an architect and from time to time, proudly showed us models of a housing estate or similar project that he had designed. He was by nature, a quiet man, never a chatty jovial uncle, but he did his best to make us happy. Occasionally, and particularly on a hot summer day, he would throw a couple of large army blankets over the washing line to make a tent for us to play in, whilst Sadie prepared sandwiches and lemonade. Aunty Sadie was a rather formidable character who, on one hand could make us quiver with fear if we incurred her displeasure, but on the other, was very kind with a sense of fun. Moreover, she loved to see us having a good time.

Visiting the Cornton was also another opportunity to play with other children from another community, when and if, aunty Sadie allowed us outside her jurisdiction. It was in the community hall in the Cornton, where the Alexander Bus Company held its annual children's Christmas party. I adored these parties because there was traditional Scottish Country Dancing, typical party food, and Santa Claus came and distributed presents.

My overriding memory of the Cornton though, is the place where I met my mother, alias 'aunty Morag', one of those secrets and lies from the cupboard of plenty. It was on a Sunday afternoon when, along with three of Isobel's children, we went to aunty Sadie and uncle Fergus's house for tea. Sadie has since told me, that she and Morag were quite close and often got up to mischief together when they were young, whilst Betty was a miserable soul who rarely saw the funny side of things. My experience living with Betty confirmed *that* statement.

When we arrived, she took me to one side and ushered me into the kitchen. Uncle Fergus, and a woman and child I had never seen before, were all seated at the table. Aunty Sadie placed her hands around my shoulders and gently moved me forwards towards the woman then asked, "Do you know who this is"? I shook my head and answered "No", to which my aunt said, "This is your mummy"!! By this time the woman had pulled me towards her, put her arm around my waist and said "Hello"! I was around nine years old and the woman, who was supposed to be my mother, had not seen me since I was around three years old. I felt absolutely nothing! The child at the table had been born a couple of years after she had abandoned Patrick, Philomena and me but whom she had kept with her.

After tea, we all went into the garden and played games, but I can remember my mother paying more attention to one of my cousins than to me. I can also remember not being in the least bothered by this. However, what was even more memorable was aunt Betty's reaction when we got home and my cousins excitedly told her that I had met my mum. The actual words she used have escaped my recollection, but the fury she expressed remains paramount in my memory. She wrote an angry letter and gave it to me to take to aunt Sadie's house the next day. When she opened it, Sadie began pacing up and down her living room reading aloud from the page "That woman, that woman, she calls her own sister, that woman!" I never found out the full contents of that letter, nor did I see my mother again throughout the rest of my childhood and adolescence. It was to be around 25yrs later before we came face to face again.

Chapter Eight

What, Every Month?

 Park Crescent was home to a number of large families, so playmates were in abundance. I was also fortunate that my extended cousins lived nearby and, because most were around my age, I was constantly in their company. As I have said, I loved being with them, especially when a new sibling came along. Without doubt, this is where my love of babies and children was nurtured. On the rare occasion when I was invited into the house of a friend whose parents did not immediately recognise me, they would say, "Oh, you must be one of Isobel's", to which I always replied, "Yes, I am". This saved me the trouble, not to mention embarrassment, of trying to explain why my surname was different, even if I did not know why myself.

Despite my small size, I do not remember any occasion when I was bullied but I suppose having a large number of relatives did mean safety in numbers. Although I had my extended cousins Moira, Cecelia, Paul, Tommy and Richard, to play with, friendships outside the family circle were still very important to me.

One of my closest friends at that time was also a classmate at St. Mary's and then later St. Modan's. Her name was Jennifer and I particularly remember how splendidly Celtic she looked with her beautiful flame coloured hair. She lived a couple of doors down the road from me and was, and maybe is still, a wonderful singer. When we were about 14 yrs old, she spent a holiday in Liverpool visiting her Aunt. On returning, she told me her Aunt and Uncle had wanted to take her to a club to sing, but her mother had been totally against the idea. She was hugely disappointed and I have often wondered if that club was the Cavern where the Beatles, Cilla Black, and other famous bands and singers had performed prior to being discovered by a record company. These were pop stars that we only ever saw on Television in Top of the Pops, therefore it would have been an excellent opportunity for Jennifer. She could sing like Lulu and could easily have been a star. We spent many happy times in her living room singing, with the obligatory hairbrush handle for a microphone, whilst her parents were out of course. My aunt however, disapproved of my friendship with her for reasons I have discovered to this day. I never told Jennifer this and continued to hang around with her, whenever possible without my aunt's knowledge. Whenever I asked aunty Betty if I could call for her, or if she came to our door asking me to come out, my aunt always said no, or would find some excuse why I could not. Despite this, Jennifer and I remained friends until I left Bannockburn to live in Stirling at the age of 18.

Another good friend who was a classmate at St. Marys lived in Hillpark. Her name was Susan and I especially loved her birthday parties because she and her sister Anne would jive and rock n' roll brilliantly. Their parents were one of the best-looking couples in the neighbourhood and had taught them to dance, so they would dance for us too. She remained one my best friends throughout our schooldays until she emigrated to Australia with her family about one year after starting at St. Modan's.

A few doors along from me lived Wendy, and her two brothers Sean and Kevin. Along with my extended cousins, I spent most of my time with them. When I have re-visited Bannockburn, I always received a warm welcome when I popped in to see Wendy, then after her marriage, her Mum and Dad. After school and during school holidays other friends consisted of children who also lived in Park Crescent but attended a different school. This was Bannockburn Primary School and then later they attended Bannockburn Secondary school. One of these friends, Heather, was a pupil at those schools, and like Susan, she emigrated to Australia in the 1960's with her family, under what became known as the £10 scheme. It was introduced via an agreement between the British and Australian governments, which allowed an entire family to move to Australia for £10 per head. However, they had to stay for around two years before they could return via the same scheme. These families became widely known throughout Australia as the '£10 Pommes'. Heather did not want to go as she did not want to leave behind her boyfriend, but as she was only 14 yrs old she had no option but to do as her parents wished. Nevertheless, after the necessary period was up, Heather came back to Scotland to live with her grandmother and later married her childhood sweetheart.

Susan on the other hand, continues to live in Perth Australia to this day. Throughout the 45yrs she has lived there, she has yearned to be back in Scotland. However, I suspect those yearnings are for the Scotland of the 1950s and '60s, than the Scotland of today.

The summer holidays between leaving St. Mary's and going to St. Modan's were particularly memorable for me. When the grass in the park had been cut, we all had enormous fun gathering it up to form huge mounds or circles. We would then find something, usually a piece of cardboard or similar, to sit on and slide down the hill and smash into the 'fort' below. On returning home in the evening hot and sweaty from all the tumbling about, I went into the bathroom for a pee, only to find that when I wiped myself, there was blood on the toilet paper. Horrified, I took this downstairs to show aunty Betty who was making jam in the kitchen with Fiona. I said "look at this, I must have got cut by a piece of glass in the grass 'cause there's blood on the paper after I wiped myself"! My aunt looked across at Fiona and said, "Will *you* tell her?"

Fiona had been a nurse before her marriage to George so I felt safe in the knowledge that she would sort this out. She took me into her bedroom and from one of her drawers, produced two huge nappy/safety pins, a stretch band of elastic webbing, and what looked to me like a 6ft. long 3 inch thick pad of cotton wool. As she placed the elastic 'thing' around my waist and the cotton wool pad between my legs, she gently explained that this bleeding was normal for a girl of my age, that the cotton wool was actually a sanitary towel and that this would happen every month and would last for a few days. I cried out "What, *every* month?", and she replied "Aye hen, *every* month". If that was not bad enough, worst was to come when she said, "Now you are like this you must not let boys touch you", and there ended my lesson on the facts of life, or the birds and the bees as we used to call it. For a long time after, if a boy should as much as brush against me during my period, I was terrified without even knowing why! I was around eleven years old. What I *did* know however was my days of tree climbing and other tomboy pursuits were now in the past.

I never knew if these 'monthly's' had happened to any of my friends. Jennifer, Susan, Heather, Wendy and me, chatted about everything under the sun, but never about *that*. Not even female family members around my own age ever discussed the subject. I was always glad though when those few days had passed, but I suspect a number of my peers were glad when theirs had arrived!

Chapter Nine

Bless me Father

Religion played a huge part in my life as it did for most Catholic families in our community during the 1950s and 60's. Confession is one element of Catholicism I am more than happy to note, is no longer compulsory. Carrying around feelings of guilt for a couple of weeks until my next confession was a heavy burden for a child. Others such as Latin Hymns, I still love to hear and am pleased to say, am still able to sing. I was perhaps, more inspired by the musical content, than the religious theme.

 I am glad to say that at that time, I did not experience the religious hatred and bigotry that my peers in Northern Ireland and arguably, parts of Scotland too, had to tolerate later. This is not to say that some bigotry did not exist. We just did not take up arms against those who had different religious beliefs from ourselves, even when an offensive remark or gesture was pointed at either section of the community. This probably sounds a very naïve statement to make, but not through the eyes of a young child from a

God fearing family living in a relatively peaceful and God-fearing community. It is to the credit of all the religious communities that this did not happen in my town throughout the years I lived there and, to this day, I am grateful for that.

Religious prejudice did however raise its ugly head in other 'minor' ways. One of the first questions a job - seeker would be asked at an interview was "Which school did you attend?" If the name of that school happened to begin with Saint, the interviewer would know immediately that the interviewee was a Catholic and if their school did not start with Saint, the interviewer would immediately assume that they were a Protestant. The job would then go to the person whose religious beliefs matched those of the interviewer. Other more important factors were taken into account, but religious denomination played its part, albeit discreetly.

It is widely known that Glasgow Celtic and Glasgow Rangers football supporters are on opposite sides of the religious divide, with Celtic consisting of mainly Catholics and Rangers mainly Protestants. Every year around New Years Day, they played each other in what was known as the 'Auld Firm' clash. After one of these clashes which Celtic happened to win, a statue of Mary, the Mother of God, was stolen from our church grounds and was found a couple of days later laying smashed to pieces in the river.

Although it was never proven, it was widely believed to have been some disgruntled and probably very drunk, Rangers supporters. Happily, I was unaware of repercussions or revenge incidents, and a replacement statue soon appeared.

The only other incident of this kind happened every year on the 12th July. This is when the Protestant members of the Grand Orange Order commemorate the defeat of the Catholic King James by the Protestant King William of Orange at the Battle of the River Boyne in 1690 in Northern Ireland. As the parade passed by our church, it would come to a halt and the drummers would perform a drum roll or beat in an act of provocation. However, and it is a credit to the Catholic community, this too did not give rise to retaliation. I used to like watching the parade as it passed our house because some of my friends were marching and I could wave to them. To a young child this was just a colourful spectacle but on one such occasion, I was prevented from watching by aunty Betty.

After a lecture on the history attached to the parade, she ordered me go and sit on the doorstep at the back of the house where I could not see it pass by. Moments later, our next-door neighbour Mrs. Ferguson saw me there, and seeing the glum look on my face, asked what was wrong. When I told her, she took me by the hand and walked with me around the side of our house, so I could see the parade without my aunt seeing me watching. One of her sons was a member of the Orange Lodge, as it was commonly known and, some years later again on the 12th July we bumped into one another, quite literally. As I was walking home from the top end of town past the local pub, he suddenly burst through the door and knocked me off the pavement and on to the road. It was late in the evening and he was so drunk he could hardly stand up. After apologising profusely, he swung his arm over my shoulder and we continued to walk in the direction of home, albeit one-step forward and two back.

In order to get him safely to his front door, we had to pass mine. Therefore all the way home, I was praying fervently to God that my aunt would have closed the curtains, so that she would not see me with a young, very drunk man draped over my shoulder, especially one who was wearing an Orange Order sash. God must have been on my side that day because the curtains were indeed closed, and I managed to put him inside the front door of his house without anyone seeing us. The incident was never mentioned by either of us again, probably because he could not remember and was perhaps too embarrassed, and I did not want it to come to the attention of Aunty Betty. What is probably now a funny episode was not so funny then. It does not bear thinking about what my aunt would have done to me had she caught sight of us. Nevertheless, we got on very well with our Protestant neighbours and they were always kind to me. Mrs. Ferguson's daughter had a German pen pal who was Catholic and when she came to visit, they asked if we would mind taking her to Mass with us, and we duly obliged.

There were times though, when there was an argument or fall-out amongst us kids, each group would call the other either Catholic Cats or Proddy Dogs. Thankfully, neither side ever won the day, so we would just get on with the game or adventure in hand. Therefore, overall religious tolerance existed in a healthy degree in our small community.

Since I loved attending school, I asked if I could join my Protestant friends at Sunday school to study and read the bible. To my dismay, I was told that I could not, and that Catholic children studied their Catechism, a form of children's bible, on a normal school day. The first lines of the Catechism went something like this:

Who made me?

God made me.

Why did God make me?

God made me to know him, to love him, and to serve him in this world, so that I would be happy with him forever in the next.

I did enjoy learning my catechism, though Sunday school had the added attraction of annual outings, and I personally took my faith seriously, attending services fervently and with enthusiasm. I revered all things 'holy' especially the Blessed Virgin Mary, Mother of God.

When I was around 6 or 7yrs old, a school playmate asked me if I was a virgin. Thinking that this was an insult to the Holy Mother, I replied with a resounding "No I am not" then promptly stomped away with an indignant air of disgust. This resulted in lots of laughter from my playmates and later my family after I relayed the 'insult' to them.

Every morning, lessons always began with prayers and woe betides anyone who made a sound or movement during them. Unfortunately, one particular morning I was bursting for a pee, but because I dare not interrupt the teacher by putting up my hand to be excused, I had to let go. My knickers, legs, socks and shoes were soaked, and I found myself standing in, what to the teacher and my classmates was a puddle but to me, felt like Loch Lomond. Fortunately, because I lived so close to our school, I was allowed to go home and change.

When we reached aged seven we were prepared by Mrs. Flaherty at the school, along with Father McAlister for our first confession. This, arguably, was the age when a child recognised right from wrong, and if a wrongdoing has been committed then the sinner has to repent. Penance usually took the form of prayer via three Hail Mary's and a good act of Contrition. Father McAlister heard confession in private in the confessional box or cubicle within the church and individuals would attend every four to six weeks.

On one such occasion, one of Isobel's children was saying his confession whilst his mother and I waited with other members of the congregation, in the pews immediately outside the cubicle. Silent prayer turned to low giggles of laughter as those present could hear him confessing to stealing some biscuits from his mother's biscuit tin. The confession ritual was the same for everyone, so must have bored poor Father Mac to distraction. Except for the sins committed of course it usually went thus, "Bless me Father for I have sinned it's ? weeks since my last confession". Most children would then say "I told lies, cheeked my elders, said bad words, that's all I remember Father". The priest would then ask us to say the prayer of contrition, whilst he proceeded to bless and forgive us. He then told us to say an Our Father i.e. The Lords Prayer and three Hail Mary's as penance. After hearing about the biscuits theft however, Father Mac must have looked towards heaven and said "Thank you Lord, something different"!

Confession was the pre-curser to receiving Holy Communion and First Holy Communion Day is a special time in Catholic children's lives. The girls looked like miniature brides in white dresses and veils and the boys looked splendid in white trousers and equally white shirts. The reasoning was that, Holy Communion could only be taken if you were free from sin. After the service and the official group photograph, a special breakfast was laid out for us in the church hall which usually consisted of sandwiches, cakes, biscuits, tea or pop. It was usual on this day to be given a present from our parents of our first set of rosary beads or a crucifix on a chain, which we would ask the priest to bless and hopefully we would keep them for ever. The following year we would be confirmed into the church. This was also a special day for us, made even more so by the attendance of our Archbishop, Joseph Gordon Gray of the diocese of St. Andrews and Edinburgh to which Bannockburn belonged, who conducted the ceremony. Some years later, he was appointed Cardinal by his holiness the Pope.

Each child chose a Confirmation name which had to be that of a saint who inspired us and whose life or good deeds we would hope to emulate. It was usually a female saint's name for the girls, a male saint's name for the boys. St. Theresa was popular amongst the girls but I chose the name Felicity. She had been a nun who was martyred a few centuries ago and was thus declared Saint Felicity. Her name was mentioned every Sunday during mass but I cannot re-call if it was really this, or her martyrdom, which inspired me to choose her.

The month of May is regarded as the month of our Lady and prayers are dedicated to her throughout the month. Each home would set aside an area for an alter, where a statue of her would take centre place surrounded with spring flowers. Ours usually consisted of jam jars with buttercups, daisies, or anything we could find growing wild at that time of year. This was a particular favourite time of year for me and I would pray to our Lady fervently. Around the age of twelve, I prayed extra hard for my long natural curls to be cut off into a more modern, straight, shorter style and to my surprise and delight my prayers were answered. However, although the length was shortened, to my horror the curls remained, as if to remind me to be careful what I prayed for as it just might be granted! Josie McKeown had been the church organist and choir leader prior to Mrs Kirkwood and even as a very young child, I appreciated and perhaps was even in awe of, his beautiful singing voice. When Josie died, the angels in heaven acquired a new and beautiful voice to sing Gods praises. It could be said he inspired me to join the choir. When I re-call my favourite hymns, it is Josie's voice I can hear singing them. St. Augustine is reputed to have said, "To sing is to pray twice". I did an awful lot of praying in those days.

I undertook collecting from the parishioners homes what was called 'The Monthly Collection' which was a voluntary donation to help with the upkeep and day to day running costs of the church. That statement is not quite true. Aunt Betty *ordered* me to volunteer the undertaking. When I took the money to Father McAlister at the chapel house, I was given a huge orange and sixpence, which would be two and a half pence in to-day's money. Moreover, even though it was known I had a collection of money on me, I was never ever robbed, mugged or threatened. Sadly, that cannot be said to-day. Sometimes the door would be answered by Father Mac himself or his housekeeper, the severe looking but kind German Miss Bergen. I often felt sorry for her because after Mass on Sunday mornings when the congregation would socialise and chat to one another, no-one chatted with her. I had concluded that maybe it was because she was German, because even though World War 2 had ended around 15 years before, memories and feelings towards Germans were still quite raw. However some years later, it was pointed out to me that she had to hurry in to the chapel house to cook Father MacAlister's breakfast so he could officiate at the next mass an hour later.

Benediction was a service usually held on Sunday afternoons and some years later, was changed to Sunday evenings. Unlike Holy Mass in the morning, it was not compulsory to attend, but I loved singing the Latin hymns so I would willingly attend. During one of these services, the priest turned around to give the usual blessing of the congregation with the holy sacramental chalice. Instead he paused, to announce that he would be unable to do so on this occasion, because there was not 12 people present. I never knew until that moment that 12 people were required to be present to receive the blessing. Although I was saddened by this, I recall being more disappointed at such a low turnout to what I believed was a more beautiful service than Mass itself. Occasionally, one of my friends would come along to the Benediction service at church on a Sunday evening. Afterwards, we would both pop into Tortellano's café for an orange drink and catch up with other friends. Of course I had to lie to my aunt as to why it took so long to get home from the service, because I was not allowed to go to the café. She had remembered it as a meeting place for the Teddy Boys some years before therefore a place to avoid, in her view by me. Another sin to confess to Father Mac perhaps, although I suspect he would have thought that going to the café in the first place, was more sinful than lying to my aunt!

Throughout the many years I have lived in England however, I have found that I no longer owe loyalty to a particular religious organisation. It could be argued, that many of my peers from the 1950s and 60's who had strong religious convictions then, may now feel the same and have found that their beliefs have become somewhat watered down. Nevertheless, I have maintained a strong belief in God and have tried to live my life, though it has to be said not 100 per cent successfully, according to the principles laid down in the Ten Commandments. I regard myself as a Christian and wherever I have lived, particularly in country villages where transport on a Sunday was non-existent, I attended a service in the Church that was nearest my home regardless of its creed. After introducing myself as a Catholic, I was without exception, made very welcome. I accept there are a number of Christian sects or groups and I respect them all. Primarily because they all share, the basic instructions laid down in the Ten Commandments, and that they are all guided by the teachings of Jesus Christ the son of God.

For around 20yrs, I have been lucky to have as a dear close friend Joanna, who is a Jehovah's Witness. We met when her eldest son started school at the same time as my youngest daughter. Our friendship began by chatting at the school gates and then progressed to sitting in her car after she had given us a lift home. When our children moved to Senior school, we continued our 'discussions' regularly over tea and cakes. Although I had informed Jo that I was born a Catholic, and would most likely die one, she continues to be my dearest friend and the best spiritual counsellor I shall ever have. Nevertheless, it is only in the recent 12 years of our friendship that I began studying the bible with her. It also has to be recorded here, that contrary to the popular belief about Jehovah's Witnesses, it was at *my* instigation, not hers. I have attended numerous services or meetings throughout those 12 years, and have met many witnesses who have humbled and inspired me. Although I no longer study on a regular basis, she is still my dearest friend and has been there for me through some difficult times with both practical help and spiritual guidance. Despite having a husband and four children to look after, she helps many in her congregation at the drop of a hat. We still have a bible get together from time to time over tea and cakes for what I call my spiritual top-up. Throughout my life, I have come across many people who call themselves Christians, but Jehovah's Witnesses are the only ones in my experience, who incorporate what the Bible teaches us, into their daily lives. I feel privileged to count them as my friends and grateful for the spiritual counsel they provide should I call upon it. Over the years, I have broadened my outlook to respect, consider, and tolerate other faiths, but a part of me will always be Catholic. That said no individual, group, or organisation should claim to have the monopoly on God. On the contrary, *he* has the monopoly on us.

St Mary's Primary First Communicants, Bannockburn

Chapter 10

Big School

Any feelings of trepidation experienced on my last day at St. Mary's soon disappeared on arrival at St. Modan's High School, Barnsdale Road, St. Ninians. The teachers, classmates and every other aspect of daily life at Primary school had been wonderful, and I found to my delight, that the ones at St. Modan's High were equally friendly, but even more inspiring. The first notably different thing between St. Mary and St. Modan's was the wearing of a school uniform. Most senior schools in the 1960s had a school uniform and what's more, most of the pupils were proud to wear it. St. Modan's, like many others, were strict about wearing it too. It consisted of Maroon blazers with the school badge in gold and white on the left breast pocket with the schools Latin motto, Modus Odens Vanos emblazoned upon it. Grey skirts, white blouses and maroon white and gold ties completed the uniform and I loved it and wore it with pride every day until the day I left. The one item of uniform I did not wear however, was the beret. It was maroon with a long golden tassel and my aunt insisted I wear it, particularly on my first day. Travelling to school by bus was a new and exciting experience, but on that first day, I noticed I was one of only a handful of pupils wearing it so I took it off, put it in my briefcase, and never wore it again.

Clarke's shoes had always been my aunty Betty's favoured footwear for all of us, probably because of their good reputation for being strong, reliable and long lasting. However, they were never looked upon as fashionable therefore I developed a real hatred for them. Although I always looked clean and smart, I always felt quite frumpy and old fashioned, particularly as cousin Isobel did not apply the same level of strictness to her daughters, of which one, Moira, was now in the same class as me. I used to envy Isobel's girls because of the relaxed attitude their mum had when it came to fashion dress code. She was more 'with it' towards them than their grandmother was with me. At the very least, they had a say in what they wore after school, whereas I did not.

Another notable difference between the schools was the segregation of the sexes into separate classes. I did not mind this one bit and I am certain the boys were of the same opinion.

As a Catholic High School, St. Modan's has consisted of pupils from a large catchment area around the county, and beyond. However, I was delighted to find that a number of my friends from St. Mary's were in the same class as me. Moreover, what I found equally delightful was, even though St. Modan's was an imposing huge, two storey building, with outside prefabricated type classrooms, I did not find it in the least intimidating. We did not have to stay in the same classroom all day like at primary school neither. Each lesson lasted approximately half an hour then at the sound of the bell we left and made our way to a different room. To children from a single story small school, this was exciting, as the corridors swarmed with maroon blazers buzzing with chatter. There was always the chance too, of bumping into friends who were not in the same class as me. The teachers looked splendid in their long black robes and some even wore their mortar board hats. Although not every teacher wore their robes, I was happy to note that most did.

My first teacher was also our form or register teacher, Miss Maureen O'Hara. She was a lovely young woman who was an ex pupil of the school and who had been in Patrick's class. She explained to us about the schools four 'houses'. Ardhattan, (red) Etive, (yellow) Kilmodan (green) and Roseneath (blue). These were like teams that consisted of pupils from all the classes in the school. They competed throughout the year for academic or sporting points and the house with most points at the end of the year received a trophy. Each house was the name of a place associated with St. Modan while he lived and preached in Scotland. It is widely believed he landed in Scotland on the shores of Loch Etive, set up a priory at Ardhattan, preached at Kilmodan, where there is also a priory and is buried at Roseneath. Initially, I was placed in Kilmodan house, but Miss O'Hara said that if anyone wanted to be in the same house as family members, past or present, then they could swap. When I found out that Patrick, Philomena and Sheena, had been in Ardhattan, I swapped. I was glad I did too, as Ardhattan were very often the winners of the school house trophy. I was glad too to find that cousin George had not been in Ardhattan, he was in Roseneath.

At St. Modan's we had subjects we never had at St. Mary's. One of those was pottery. Art was, and still is, amongst my worst subjects, as I cannot draw not even if my life depended on it. I was so bad, that if I had taken up painting for a living I would have died of hunger within a week. However, I was good at making things, so when we made medallions in pottery class I was so pleased with mine, that I wore it around my neck to school the following day. Unfortunately, this was a day the headmaster Mr. McCann, decided to call in to speak with Miss O'Hara. As he reached to open the door on his way out, he turned and noticing me in the first desk by the door, saw the medallion around my neck. Pointing to it he asked, "what is this?" to which I replied with more than a hint of pride in my voice, "I made it in Art class sir". Thinking he was about to compliment me on my beautiful handicraft work, I was soon choking on the said pride when he said, "Well take it off, you don't wear things like that with your school uniform"! That was my very first encounter with my senior school headmaster and sadly, would not be my last.

Another subject which was new to us was domestic science. Of course, a sign of the times, this subject was solely for girls, whereas boys had lessons in woodwork. An internal part of the school building had been set aside to replicate a flat, or house. It consisted of a kitchen, sitting room, dining room, bathroom and bedroom. They were scaled down models of the real thing, intended to teach us girls how to clean and cook, thereby preparing us for our lives as future wives and mothers. Our domestic science teacher was a young woman named Miss Burr, who always insisted we pronounce her name properly i.e. Burr not Bur! She taught us every aspect of the subject, from how to clean a hairbrush to cooking a hot meal. One day, my friend Susan and I were told to clean the bathroom, whilst the rest of our classmates were given other tasks. As the bathroom door could be conveniently (pardon the pun) locked from the inside and had frosted glass, we locked ourselves in and spent the entire lesson sitting chatting. Much to our delight, Miss Burr hadn't even missed us!!

Miss Mitchell was our PE teacher. She was sweet and, besides the usual gymnastic exercises, taught us netball and hockey. As this was our first year, most of us were aged around 11 and still wearing vests, or so I thought. When lining up to play hockey one day, I looked along the row of white blouses and noticed one or two girls were wearing nylon see-through blouses like mine. However, it was not a vest that showed through *their* blouses, but a bra. I was mortified to have a vest showing through mine, so as soon as I got home from school I asked my aunty Betty if I could have a bra. After roars of laughter from both her and Isobel who had called in for a visit, she replied, "what dae ye want a bra fur? Ye've nothin' tae put in it." She decided I could not have one for a long time yet, so I did not wear a nylon blouse for P.E. ever again.

Whilst Miss Mitchell was alright with us girls, the boys were not so fortunate with their P.E. teacher, Mr. Murphy, or as we all called him, 'spud' Murphy. If a class of boys were lined up beside us girls waiting to go into the changing rooms, he would often single out a couple of boys in order to humiliate them in front of us. I found this particularly nasty and did not like the man because of that. However, I have recently found on the 'Friends re-

United' web-site, a number of favourable comments about him from past male pupils. This however, has just reinforced my belief that his humiliation of the boys only took place in front of us girls for the benefit of his ego.

Occasionally, we shy quiet first years had to share the changing room with another class. Unfortunately for us they were a particularly noisy class and on one extra noisy day when Miss Mitchell was unable to control them, Mr. McCann came storming into the changing room. His face was red with rage, as he bellowed out "I can hear this noisy bad behaviour from my office at the other end of the corridor". He then ordered all of us to wait outside his office in a line of twos, with cries of "Please sur, it wasnae us", falling on deaf ears. I was first in the queue and after giving me a good hard smack on the hand with his thick leather strap, he told me to go to the back and when I reached the front again, repeated the exercise once more. That was my second encounter with the Headmaster of my senior school, but the third and final one was to take place three or four years later and was just as painful, although not in a physical sense.

Those two unfortunate encounters with the Headmaster in my first year at big school did not douse my enthusiasm for the establishment and I eagerly attended most of my lessons: with perhaps less enthusiasm for Maths and Science. Nevertheless, I did enjoy some science lessons, especially when experiments were conducted even though sadly, I was not very good at them. Typing and shorthand were fascinating and I enjoyed them enormously. Geography too, took me to places and covered issues more interesting than the basic curriculum of Primary school. However, History, Music, and English were the subjects that for me, reigned supreme.

Chapter 11

It Wasnae Me!

Whilst the changes taking place in my school life were happy and exciting, life at home continued to produce trials and tribulations that had a profound effect on me. One particular incident left me so emotionally scarred that its consequences remain with me even to the present day. It concerned an amount of money that had gone missing from Isobel's house. The houses in our neighbourhood had coin meters whereby shilling (ten pence today) coins were fed into it to pay for the electricity used by the household. Every so often a representative from the electric board commonly known as the 'Meter Man' came to empty the meter. He calculated how much electricity was used, against how many shillings were collected in the meter then, returned any excess shillings to the householder. Isobel had stacked the returned shillings on the sideboard in bundles of 20, each bundle adding up to £1, but on this occasion, one of the bundles was missing. After a process of elimination had taken place, it became clear that the culprit or thief was either Isobel's daughter Moira, or me. I knew I had not taken them and protested my innocence profusely, but to my horror and dismay, so did Moira. The 'trial' took place in the courthouse of the living room in my house, the jury consisting of aunty Betty, Isobel, George and Fiona. With neither of us owning up to the theft, it was suggested that Moira and I should go on an errand to the Co-op at hill park to fetch a loaf of bread, and by the time we had returned, one of us would own up. That was perhaps the strangest errand I had ever been sent on in my life because, all the way there and back, not a word of coherent conversation took place between us. The only clear words I can recall were, "Wis it you?" "Naw!" "Well it wasnae me!"

When we returned and neither of us had owned up, Isobel took Moira home whilst Betty, George, and Fiona, all searched every inch of my bedroom. They emptied all my drawers, upturned the mattress on my bed; where they found posters of my favourite pop idols, The Beatles, Walker Brothers et al, (I was not allowed to put them on the wall) along with pictures of Glasgow Celtic football team. Aunty Betty angrily threw them out the bedroom window and burned or binned them later. During this onslaught into my deeply personal belongings, to the familiar chorus of "Jist like yer mither", I was trembling with a mixture of fear and anger. However, I must have protested too much, because I was slapped so hard across my face by 'he who must be in control' George, that I fell back onto my bed sobbing. Typically, this all happened whilst there was no one to defend me. Patrick was still in the Navy, Philomena was at work, and Sheena and Hamish were miles away in another town. When it was clear that the money was not in my room, George bellowed at me to tidy up and not come downstairs until told to do so.

Later that evening when we were all sitting round the table having tea, Isobel came in. She went into the living room to speak to her mother, informed her that Moira had owned up to stealing the money, then went home again and that was the end of the matter. Not one word of apology to me was forthcoming from anyone, including Moira. As a direct consequence of that episode, I have been unable to work in a place that involved money. For example whenever an opportunity arose to work in a shop, bank, or pub, I declined for fear if any money went missing, my seniors would blame me. It became apparent some years later, that my mother had been a bit of a kleptomaniac, so they assumed, like mother, like daughter.

Another profound incident that remains etched in my memory was the day Isobel and Jock had a fall-out. I had called down to their house as I did on a countless number of times, and when I walked in to the living room, a couple of my cousins were crying. When I asked what was wrong Moira, through her tears, said that Isobel and Jock had argued and after a terrible row, Isobel stormed out and headed for her sister-in law's house about ten minutes walk away. At this I too began to cry, then one of the older children turned to me and said "I dinnae ken why *you're* greetin', she's no' your mammy"! I turned around and fled the house, sobbing all the way home. They were right of course, she was not my mother and I knew that, but since the age of around five when Granny died, I had kind of 'shared her' with them and she had always allowed me to call her 'Mammy'. I had felt their sadness at the thought of her leaving, but this was the first time anyone had actually spoken the words that made it painfully clear I did not have a mother of my own.

Thankfully, she returned in time for the younger children's bedtime and everything returned to normal, but I can honestly say that was the one and only time I recall them having such an argument. In those days, most couples would have their blowouts then just get on with things, although clearly, this was not the case in *my* mum and dad's relationship. Another highly emotive incident came one day as I was attending to my aunt who was in bed with one of her usual ailments. Cousin Isobel was sitting by the bedside chatting with her when I unexpectedly asked, "Where's my Dad?" I was around 14 years old and although I had acquired a vague understanding regarding my mother; even though it had never been properly explained to me; my father was never mentioned. I did not know his name, nor if he was alive or dead. Even throughout my childhood, the knowledge that Isobel's children had Jock as their father, never invoked a desire to ask where my own father was. Women had been the dominant elders in my family life for as long as I could remember, and male family members only consisted of brother, cousin, or uncle. Curiosity over a missing father figure, protector, and provider was sure to get the better of me one day, and that day had arrived. However, I was unprepared for the answer when I did summon up the courage to ask the dreaded question. "Where's ma Dad?"

The words had no sooner poured from my mouth when I thought, "Aw naw, noo I'm goin' tae get a belt". Both Betty and Isobel could not have looked more shocked if I had said a nuclear bomb has just been dropped on Stirling! There was so much shouting coming from them that the only response that remained embedded in my memory is "Have ye got a dirty mind or somethin'?" "Whit dae ye want tae ken that fur?" Translated means, "Have you got a dirty mind or something"? Why do you want to know that?" That was the first and last time the subject of my legitimacy arose, and the question remained unanswered for many more years. Of course unknown to me at that time, I was one of only two of our granny's seven grandchildren who *were* legitimate! Isobel was the other one.

That wonderful day finally arrived when cousin George, Fiona and their two children got the keys to their own home. It was a beautiful newly built council flat at the top end of town. There were only three blocks of five or six storey flats, unlike the numerous huge tower blocks found in many of the larger towns. Although ecstatic to see *him* leave, I was equally sad to see Fiona and the children go. I had become particularly close to his youngest daughter from when she was a tiny baby, and although I knew we would still see one another regularly, I was going to miss both children's presence in the house very much. Moreover, I was going to miss Fiona, and not just because she did most of the household chores whilst I was at school and Philomena was at work. It was great having her around, and she always greeted me home from school with a welcoming smile and a cheery 'Hello'. Best of all though, she would on occasion, stand up for me against George.

Chapter 12

Respite

With Patrick away most of the time in the navy, there was now only Betty, Philomena and I living in the house. Although the fear of living in the same house as my cousin had gone, the downside was that I would no longer come home from school to a lovely warm, tidy house, blazing fire, and the wonderful aroma of the evening meal on the cooker. I was the first one home at the end of the day, which was not too bad in summer, but during the winter the house was so cold I could see my own breath.

My first chore was to get the living room fire going. The ashes from the fireplace had to be cleaned out to make way for scrunched up sheets of old newspaper, a few chopped sticks of kindling wood, covered by small pieces of coal, before it could be lit. Apart from heating the living room, this fire heated the water tank that supplied the house with hot water. This daily schedule meant that by the time Philomena and aunty Betty arrived home, the water would be piping hot, the living room warm and I would have peeled the potatoes for tea along with one or two other household chores. Sometimes though, before scrunching up the newspaper, I would be tempted to read an article or two and before I knew it, I had read the entire newspaper. Consequently, they would both arrive home to a cold living room and no hot water, thereby resulting in a good tongue-lashing for me.

 Even though there was now only three of us in the house at this time, every room had to be cleaned regularly in military precision, all seven of them. Bathroom, three bedrooms, upstairs sitting room, downstairs living room, kitchen, along with the landing, hall, and stairs, were cleaned in an operation similar to that of painting the Forth Bridge. No sooner had the whole house been cleaned, we would start all over again. Weekends were when the bulk of the housework was done and Sunday was no exception. Saturday would find my sister and me washing, ironing, hoovering, and food shopping. On Sunday mornings after Mass, we polished the furniture and whenever I smell Mansion furniture polish, it takes me back to a Sunday morning in that house. Whilst our aunt was cooking Sunday lunch, we were busy working away whilst listening to two-way family favourites on the radio with Cliff Mitchellmore and Jean Metcalfe. This was a popular ritual in many households but more so in our house as it included requests for and from, men and women serving in the forces. Under the heading of B.F.P.O., which

I believe, stood for British Forces Personnel Overseas, (but I could stand corrected) they were military bases in Germany, Cyprus, and Gibraltar that linked up with the UK via the BBC. This enabled families to send in requests for a song for their relative serving there and vice versa. I was always on full alert during this programme in case a request came on for us from my brother, sadly it never did. When my daily chores were completed, and I was free to go out and see my friends, I was often too tired or they had gone off somewhere.

Respite from this schedule however, came when Sheena's husband Hamish, began a new job in the Manor Powys coalmine near Alloa a few miles east of Stirling. This required him to work night shift for four or five nights every third week and, as she did not want to sleep on her own on these nights, she asked aunty Betty if I could stay with her. They came to collect me in their car on a Sunday evening and I returned home after school on Friday afternoon. Into my school briefcase, I had to pack the schoolbooks required for the week, P.E. kit, a change of white blouse, socks, underwear, along with personal items. That briefcase could put Mary Poppins' carpetbag to shame with the amount of school and non-school items that could fit in it. There was also the added advantage of aunty Betty being unaware of what I put in to take with me.

One Sunday evening, Hamish announced that he had acquired his family's young black Labrador dog. Unfortunately, his first night in their house coincided with Hamish's night shift, and as my cousin and I were not familiar with him nor he us, we approached him rather warily. He decided during the night that he was rather lonely downstairs on his own so he came upstairs, jumped on the bed, lay across our legs and fell asleep. In the darkness, I could hear Sheena whispering to me "Dinnae move an inch in case he goes fur us". Therefore, we spent the whole night partly stiff with fear, that he might attack us, and physically stiff because he was so heavy our legs were numb and we could no longer feel them! When Hamish arrived home the next morning he laughed and said, "Ye pair 'o wallys, he's as saft as a brush and widnae hurt a flea" then added, "He was taking advantage o' ye's". He was never allowed on the bed again.

Whenever Sheena sent me to the shops, he came with me and carried my shopping basket in his mouth, and even when it was quite heavy, he was determined to carry it. Although I was not well known in this neighbourhood, local people instantly recognised him and would say "Hello Bruce". Some years later, I was very sad to learn that he died of poisoning, possibly by a cruel neighbour.

From time to time, I called in to Sheena's shoe shop to wait until she had finished work, then we would get the Alloa bus to her house. On one of those occasions, she asked me to help her carry a sun lamp that one of her colleagues had loaned her. This was probably the pre-curser of a sun bed and we were both eager to try it out. That evening after we set it up, she said that I could have a go under it first. Wow! I was thrilled to bits at the thought of turning up for the school bus the next morning sporting a glowing tan. She did not have a go herself as she thought she would wait and see how I looked first. The term 'guinea pig' did not enter my mind at that point! I probably would not have cared anyway, because to me, her word was gospel. So there I was, standing at the school bus stop on a snowy January morning with a face the colour of a Sioux Indian, beetroot, and embarrassment all rolled into one! Of course, my beloved cousin had decided not to go under it after all! I loved those times staying there, not just because I was away from that house and aunty Betty, but also because I loved being around Sheena and Hamish. They always treated me with kindness and love and I look upon that part of home-life, as the only times during my adolescence that I was truly happy. It is also true to say that it was thanks to Sheena's presence in my life that I survived the whole period with some semblance of sanity, because aunty Betty was turning into a bigger bully than her son had ever been.

The numbers in our household dwindled even further when, not long after George and his family moved out, Philomena also left home. Like others before her, it began with an argument with the matriarchal Betty. Philomena had fallen pregnant and she and her boyfriend wanted to marry. My presence was not required at the Inquisition held by senior family members regarding her 'state'. Her boyfriend along with his parents came to our house to discuss the marriage arrangements. Betty insisted I get out of the house until they had left but I felt quite sorry for her, as she looked quite vulnerable in the lions den, and wished I could have stayed if just for moral support. When they allowed me back into the house, her boyfriend and his parents had left and had taken Philomena with them. No one explained to me the content or outcome of the 'discussion', but by Betty's anger as she strode back and forth across the living room floor, I guessed. Besides, I had seen that rage and pace on previous occasions, and it usually meant that she was not having things her own way. A few days later uncle Fergus came with Philomena and helped move her things out. She was going to live with her future in-laws, which was I suspect, had been the real stinging point of the discussion. In a practical sense, our house was the ideal place for them to begin married life and to have their baby. Spare rooms, a handy bus route for work, live-in babysitter, would have been a huge help for them, and a financial contribution to the household would have provided extra help for aunty Betty. However, it was and still is my belief that she rejected the idea so she could get away from that house, and our domineering aunt. I for one could not blame her, therefore yet another family wedding was to take place without good representation from our side. George approached me some time before the wedding, to tell me she had asked permission that I be bridesmaid, insisting that it was up to me if I chose to go or not. I was so shocked at not only been given the choice, but spoken to as a human being by him, that I stammered "You only want me to go so you can all give me the third degree when I get home regarding who said what about whom". He replied that they would not, but I refused to believe him and that was the reason I did not attend my sister's wedding. A number of years earlier, Patrick had married the sister of one of his shipmates in Cornwall. Aunty Sadie and uncle Fergus, Sheena and Hamish along with Philomena who was bridesmaid, all travelled south for the ceremony. I was not asked to go therefore did not attend his wedding neither. I was heartbroken at the time and felt left out. It was at times like these that the feelings of loneliness, of being unimportant, were at their most profound. However, that marriage only lasted a couple of years because, whilst he was away with the navy in Borneo, she left him.

Chapter 13

St. Modan's Revisited

Towards the end of my first year at St. Modan's, the school authorities announced that a number of forms/classes were to be moved to the old Stirling High School premises in Stirling old town. However, some subjects currently taught at the main school in St. Ninians were not to be taught in Stirling. In order for me to continue in my chosen subjects, especially French and Intensive Commercial (today's equivalent of Business Studies), and continue at the main school in St. Ninian's, I was told I would have to repeat the first year. As I was one of the youngest in my class, there would not be a problem and my aunt had decided I was not going up to Stirling in any case. The blow of parting with my new classmates diminished when I found one or two others would be staying too.

It turned out to be one of those rare decisions made on my behalf by Aunty Betty, which made me very happy, as it was in this class 1E, where I met amongst others, Rena Welby, Elizabeth Lawther, Anne Heaney, Teresa Lennon, Amanda Notreangelo, and Teresa Gineandrea. Although none of them lived in Bannockburn, these girls became my very best friends and I loved every minute I spent with them. As I was the only one of our group who went home at lunchtime, I would race like mad to get back in order to spend time with them before the afternoon classes began. Occasionally I would wriggle out of going home and stayed at school. I spent my bus fare on sweets such as chocolate MB bars, or a bag of spearmints and we would walk up to the grassy hill of the Borestone, especially on warm sunny days and just sit and chill out there.

During one such lunchtime, we watched aghast as a small plane flew overhead in the direction of the Ochil Hills with smoke billowing from its tail. Moments before it disappeared from view, what appeared to be a parachute came floating downwards. Like the good conscientious citizens that we were, we dialled 999 with Rena as spokesperson, and informed the police of a plane crash and the pilot bailing out over the hills. Feeling quite pleased with ourselves that our actions had probably saved the pilots life, we relayed the story over and over to everyone in school all afternoon. We were all anxious to get home from school so we could re-tell it to our families. However, when Rena arrived home a journalist from The Scotsman newspaper was waiting with her mortified mother in their living room. She had given the police her name and address and they in turn, after investigating the report, had informed the newspaper, who then sent a reporter to Rena's home to interview her.

After a thorough search of the entire area by all the rescue services, including Mountain Rescue teams, no plane, not even the wreckage of one, nor parachutist either alive or dead, was found. To say we were mortified would be putting it mildly, not only within our families, but also to the entire school the next day. We were hugely embarrassed to find that the paper had printed our report of the 'ghost plane over the Ochils' in its evening edition. To this day, we never did find out exactly what it was that we *did* see, but five of us knew it was no ghost! For a couple of days though, we felt like 'The Famous Five', or maybe it was 'The Infamous Five'!

Although the wearing of school uniform was sacred, occasionally a fashion item would appear where so many were wearing it, that the school authorities would have had a rebellion on their hands had they tried to forbid it. One example was during the early years of The Beatles when it seemed *everything,* such as mugs, notebooks, ties and numerous other items had pictures of the group on them. If an item did not have a picture of the Fab Four on it, there would be beetles of the insect kind portrayed instead. The fashion item we wore to school was tights, which had tiny beetles patterned all over. It would take more than a thrashing with the headmasters strap to stop us girls from wearing those tights. I was pleasantly surprised when aunty Betty allowed me to wear them from time to time! Perhaps that was because they were quite thick and thus warm on cold days. Mary Quant had designed the min-skirt, so like true followers of fashion and to the horror of the teachers, we rolled over the elastic waistbands of our grey school skirts to the required short length then, unrolled them again before reaching home. Besides new friends, I also encountered new teachers. My favourite teacher of all was without doubt Miss McNamee and not only because she taught my favourite subject of History, but because she was a lovely sweet person too. Not a soft touch, but softly spoken with a mild gentle demeanour. The actor Penelope Keith reminds me of her. She did a lot of writing on the blackboard so we could copy it into our exercise books and as I loved the act of writing, this appealed to me enormously. However, it also meant that the board duster got quite chalky, so to clean it she would take a ruler, open a window and lean out to tap of the chalk dust. Our history classroom was on the upper floor of the school, and if there were a breeze, the chalk dust came flying back in and covered her. The expression on her face was priceless and we could not help but giggle. Nevertheless, she was an inspiration to me and I am sure to many more pupils who followed.

Miss McNamee gave me a lifelong love of History and although I regrettably, did not make it my career, I was offered a place as a mature student at both Sheffield Universities to study for a B.A. in History. The course at Sheffield University was on Social History, but I accepted the offer from Sheffield Hallam University, because their course was more diverse, covering Social, Political, Economic, and Cultural history over the last two Centuries. As a mature student, wife, and mother of three, I chose part-time study, which meant I had to pay the fees, and it would take six years to complete the degree. Personal circumstances however, dictated I could only complete the first full year of study, over two years. I was therefore, unable to complete my degree, but the History department have written to tell me that there will always be a place for me should I decide to return. Who knows, maybe one day? Ultimately, I have to thank Miss McNamee for introducing me to the colourful, exciting events and characters that make up our past. Through that introduction, I have acquired a thirst for historical knowledge that continues to rage until this day. I was extremely pleased to hear that she eventually became headmistress of the school.

If Miss McNamee was my favourite teacher, Miss Neil our music teacher, ran a very close second. She was an attractive young woman with a modern dress sense, and when she walked along the corridor with her handbag tucked under her arm chewing gum, we thought she was 'cool'. Like Miss McNamee, she left a lasting impression on me with regard to her subject, music. She introduced me to classical music, besides the bog standard pieces I was learning at piano lessons. For example Johann Strauss', The Blue

Danube, How Beautiful Are the Feet from Handel's Messiah, Who is Sylvia, The Alleluia Chorus, to name just a few. The one song that features strongly in my memory however, is "Oh Had I Jubal's Lyre" from Exsultate Jubilate by Mozart. This song was quite difficult to sing as it involved holding a number of notes on one breath. Nevertheless, I am proud to say I could do it and on more than one occasion, Miss Neil would ask me to stand up and sing it to the class. For the end of school year concert and prize-giving ceremony, she chose our class to represent the first year. We were a smash hit, everyone loved us, and even teachers who did not normally teach us, stopped us in the corridor the next day exclaiming how good they thought we were. I was saddened, but not surprised that none of the adults from my family had attended the event, but news of our success had filtered through the grapevine back home, which earned me a most unusual nod of approval from Betty.

Miss Neil taught me the art of breathing properly, stomach muscle control, advice on how to avoid singing through the nose, pronouncing the vowels clearly and other techniques. These all stood me in good stead when I joined the church choir, sang at gatherings, and later in my life when I sang in public with my future husband. It came as no surprise when I learned that I had been born into a musical family. My grandfather had played clarinet in an orchestra and aunty Sadie, along with my mother, could play piano and both were considered to be very good singers.

Moreover, I have passed the love of singing on to my children. When they were young, we would prance around the house in single file singing the now classic songs from musicals like, The Sound of Music, Calamity Jane, Oliver and too many more to mention. Musical talent runs in their father's family too. His grandmother had been a good singer and both she and his mother, were very good pianists. He himself plays guitar and is an excellent singer, and it has made us both very happy to see our daughters with musical abilities and talents. One of our girls passed an audition to become a member of The Sheffield Junior Girls Choir and has now carved out a career as a singer/songwriter in L.A. California. She has provided vocals, and writes and co-writes, for bands and individual artistes in Nashville. Prior to her musical career, she gained a Diploma in Fashion Design and Technology, at the London College of Fashion.

Another of our daughters was for a time a DJ, and she wrote, co-wrote, and recorded a number of songs while living in New York, for the nightclub dance scene. A number had airtime on national Radio in the UK and she performed as far afield as Moscow. Besides this, both she and our youngest daughter are currently involved in operating a DJ agency.

Although musical talent is in my genes, I have to say without doubt, Miss Neil brought it to the fore and I thank her most sincerely for that.

Another of my teachers remains in my memory more for personal than tutorial reasons. His name was Mr. (Ronnie) O'Reilly and though he was a very good teacher in his subject of Science, sadly this was not one of my best ones. Aunty Betty is his Godmother, and from time to time, his parents came to visit, which meant I would have to serve tea, or percolated coffee and sandwiches. This meant I had to bring out the best china, wash and dry it, make the usual salmon sandwiches and act as waiter. I suppose it could be said that this was a good opportunity to show off what I had learned in Miss Burr's class, but alas no, I had learned from an earlier age than most of my peers, how to cook, clean and play host.

While I was at St. Modan's I, and a number of other pupils had the opportunity to have piano lessons. The cost was shared equally between the education department and the pupil. What's more, they took place in school lesson time, which suited both aunty Betty and me. They took place once a fortnight and the lessons I had to miss to accommodate them, were one History and one Music lesson, both of which I could easily catch up on. Mrs. Davies was the teacher and she only came to the school to provide piano lessons a couple of days each week. One day Mrs. Davies said to me "I don't normally teach pupils in my own home, but if your aunt will agree, I would like to teach you there." I am ashamed to say that I told her my aunt had said no, when in fact I had not even asked her. Another one for Father Mac perhaps? Although I enjoyed playing classical music on the piano, I had become more interested in the Beatles and other kinds of pop music of the era, so I began to resent spending my spare time going for piano lessons. However, as my love of classical music developed over later years, I regretted that resentment. If the opportunity to have singing lessons had arisen, I would have jumped at the chance, but I had not told anyone of this preference so it never arose.

A family gathering took place whereupon the chance to mention my preference did arise. It was during a party at Isobel's house to celebrate the christening of her eldest son Ian's first child. There were a number of relatives from both her and Jock's side of the family, which meant some were Catholic and some Protestant. We all sat around the room and each took a turn to provide entertainment. When it was my turn, I asked if it would be acceptable to sing an Irish rebel song called The Dying Rebel, given the mixed audience. The Protestant relatives had no problem with that whatsoever and gave their blessing. I did not realise at the time the irony of my choice of song, because I had not known then my father came from

Dublin, which meant that I was half-Irish, and he was a boy at the time of Irelands struggle for Independence from Britain. There must have been a few uncomfortable bums sitting on those chairs that evening.

When I had finished, everyone said what a lovely singer I was and Ian turned to me and said, "That was lovely, wouldn't you like to have singing lessons?" Ian was a particular favourite cousin so I was especially pleased he had liked my singing. I replied that I would love to, but although we were in my aunt's earshot, she did not comment and the subject never arose again. It was pointless asking because I knew Betty would not have given her permission. One evening, I overheard her referring to me saying, "That's one thing I'll say aboot hur, she never asks for anythin". Too true, because I knew I would not get it so there was no point in asking!

Another form/register teacher I remember with fondness was Mrs.Olzock. I may have misspelled her name, for which I sincerely apologise. Her nickname was inevitably, Mrs. auld sock and she taught Biology. My abiding memory of her however, is that in the 1960s she taught us the school song/hymn 'Hail! St. Modan'. Some have said that she either wrote or co-wrote it. When Miss Neil chose our class to represent the first years to sing at the Albert Hall, she asked Mrs. Olzock to come and hear us practice. She was so proud of us she looked as though she would burst into tears.

It was typical of almost all the teachers to care about us. They wanted us to excel in whatever way suited our capabilities and, judging by accounts I have read on the Friends Re-United web-site et al, the current staff at St. Modan's still do to-day.

Chapter 14

The Wage Earner

The lowest point of my school life and the third and final encounter with Mr. McCann came in February 1965, during my third year. Aunty Betty was reading The Stirling Observer newspaper when she spotted a job vacancy and told me to apply for it. This was a hammer blow, completely unexpected, and shook me to the core. I had turned the legal school leaving age at that time of 15 just a few weeks previously, and she had agreed that I could stay on to study Intensive Commercial in the fourth year. However, on seeing the job vacancy as a clerical assistant at the Co-operative offices in Stirling, she decided I should apply for it in order to bring in another wage to supplement that of Philomena's and her own. No matter how much I protested, the writing pad and pen was slammed down onto the table, and Philomena frog marched me over to write out an application.

I defiantly did my utmost to use bad grammar and spelling mistakes, but to no avail. Three attempts were torn up, and thrown onto the fire. By the fourth attempt my sister, who was becoming more and exasperated, exclaimed, "In the name o' God and fur the sake o' piece, will ye write it oot properly!" Then she whispered, "Ye might no' get the job". It was with that thought in mind, albeit with a heavy heart, I wrote it neatly. Subsequently, I was asked to attend an interview and as I was about to enter the Managing Director's office, through the open door of an adjoining room I saw a familiar face. The Board of Directors had gathered for a meeting and one of them was Mr. O'Reilly Senior, father of Ronnie. "That's it," I thought, "They're going to offer me the job" and my heart sank. Sure enough, they offered me the job, and I had to call on my inner strength to stop me from crying on the bus on the way home. As I approached our house, I bumped into Elizabeth Preston, a childhood playmate from a few doors down the road. Through sobs and tears, I blurted out to her my dismay at having to leave school. She was delighted I had been successful in obtaining a job, but offered her sympathy because I had to leave school.

Next day, I had to report to the Headmaster my intention to leave school as I had found employment. He must have sensed my anguish, because he gently put his arm around my shoulder and asked "Now are you sure you want to leave?" Unable to look him in the eye I replied "Yes Sir", mentally noting another one for Father Mac. That moment was as painful for me than if he had taken out his leather strap and whacked me across my hands. Of course I had lied, because I most certainly did *not* want to leave school. If I had answered "No Sir" it most certainly would have set the wheels in motion for an inquisition the medieval Spanish would have envied, thus making my life at home not worth living. After leaving Mr. McCann's office, I had to inform my teachers of 'my' decision. By this time, my anguish was obvious and they knew that my sorrow at leaving school was genuine. Every one of them was truly sorry, but it was Miss Ferguson our French teacher, whose words I remember most when she said "Oh dear, just as you were coming along nicely with your French too". She had summed up my progress in most of the subjects I was studying, thus the teachers had all expected me to do reasonably well in the end of year exams. I pleaded with aunty Betty for a compromise to stay on at school at least until May. That was when the Junior Leaving Certificate exam took place, which would at least have given me some kind of record of achievement, but she would not budge. Therefore, I left school with nothing to show for my academic efforts and a broken heart at leaving my friends.

My first day at work happened to fall on a Wednesday. Therefore, I went from wearing a school uniform complete with ankle socks one day, to wearing a hand-knitted jumper, straight skirt and stockings, the next. The compulsory Clarke's sandal type shoes that I had been wearing to school only the day before completed the ensemble. I was more than aware of the look of pity, along with the occasional giggle, from my new colleagues as they eyed me from head to toe on that first day. Betty did not allow me to wear a suspender belt, so I had to wear garters, the homemade kind of course. These were made of strips of grey elastic, which was usually sold on a piece of card and bought by mums to hold up their children's knee high socks. Two lengths were cut to fit around the tops of my legs, to hold up my stockings and prevent them from falling down around my ankles. I was not alone in my condemnation of these homemade 'accessories'. Many a poor woman's elastic garters snapped whilst walking along the street then, with excruciating embarrassment, they would take off their shoe to remove the stocking and place it in their handbag or pocket. The hardest part of this exercise was to walk on as though nothing had happened! I was extremely happy when some months later I acquired a suspender belt to hold them up. However, the crème de la crème came later with the arrival of nylon tights. The happiness that greeted these items was too immense to describe here. 'Sheer Bliss' some would say, 'Heaven' said others, but most women agreed that they were 'The best thing since sliced bread'! At the end of each day, those strips of grey elastic had left a bright red indentation around the top of both legs, and it still puzzles me to this day, how they managed to move at all, with such little blood circulating around them.

Nevertheless, mine did move albeit reluctantly, to the Stirling Co-operative offices at Pitt Terrace in Stirling. My wages were £4. 6/8d. per week, around

£4.60p in today's money, all of which I handed over to my aunt. These were the days when in most households, 21 was the age you acquired independence and became an adult in your own right, or 'came of age' as it was commonly known. An agreed amount of 'Dig' money from your wages was paid to your parents for board or 'keep' and the rest was your own, to do with what you liked. Although some families had begun to be more lenient with their offspring before this age, no degree of emancipation had arrived in our house. From my wages, my aunt gave me 12/6d, about 62p, to cover my work costs and personal needs. A weekly bus ticket cost 7/6 about 37p, leaving 5/- about 25p, for stockings, or tights, contribution to the office tea kitty, and anything else I should require over and above my meals. There was never enough left for outings such as pictures or dancing, or even new clothes. Not that it mattered much because I was rarely allowed to go out, and in any case, aunty Betty picked the clothes I wore.

My wardrobe consisted of a number of my sister's hand-me-down clothes such as jumpers and skirts that were thankfully, in good condition because like Sheena, she looked after her clothes. The downside of this was, because my sister was five years older than me, her clothes were old fashioned, so I looked and felt very frumpy in them. Handing clothes down to siblings was a common practice within a number of families of the 1960s, but five years was then and still is today, a very long time in the world of fashion. A large number of fashion statements can come and go during that period. Therefore, to a young 15year old, this was highly embarrassing.

Customers who shopped at the Co-op usually became a member or shareholder, and had a share, or check number. Each time they bought something from any department of the Co-op, they would tell the shop assistant their number, he or she would write it in the 'check book', then hand the customer a duplicate copy. This was their record of how much they had spent. When these books arrived at our office, we would tear out the slips and arrange them in bundles of their own individual number. Every financial quarter these recorded amounts when added together, determined the amount of dividend that was paid out, according to the percentage applicable at the time. This practice became known affectionately as 'The Divvy'. It ceased many years ago, but there are many people over the age of around 50, who like me, can still remember their family's share number today.

My role in the office during 'The Divvy' payout was to go downstairs to the Public Office and, on receipt of their share book, give the shareholders the slip of paper that told them how much dividend they would receive. They then walked over to my colleagues behind the counter, to collect their money.

One day, a shareholder came in without his little black share book so I refused to pass him his collection slip. He said,"Do you know who I am?" To which I replied, "No sir, I don't know who you are, but even if I did, I still cannot give you your slip without your share book!" Throughout this verbal exchange, my colleagues behind the counter were giggling and whispering to one another. He replied, "I am the managing director of the Co-op", and then he turned to my colleagues and said, "She is only doing her job!" Before leaving, without the slip I might add, he told me not to worry as I had acted correctly. It was a laughing point in the staff room, but somehow I think I had the last laugh.

Apart from my first place of work, the Co-op offices were also the place where I smoked my first cigarette. According to my peers, many had their first cigarette whilst still at school, usually behind the bike sheds or in the toilets, but I was never remotely interested in smoking. I was so anti-smoking, I used to chastise Philomena when, from time to time, she would light up a cigarette whilst our aunt was out, exhaling the smoke up the chimney so she would not detect the smell. However, during a tea break one morning, a colleague asked me if I smoked and when I replied that I had never tried it, she offered me a puff of hers. It made me feel quite sick and light headed, so I decided never to have one again. A couple of years later I tried again and consequently became a regular smoker. Throughout the rest of my life, I had an on off relationship with the dreaded weed, finally ending the relationship for good in my fifties.

Now there was only the two of us in the house, my life was becoming almost unbearable as I became the full focus of aunty Betty's undivided attention. Before I left for work she would check me over to make sure I was wearing her choice of clothes. One morning she did not like the way I had styled my hair so she angrily grabbed the hairbrush from my hand and brushed it for me, with backward sweeping strokes that left me looking as though I had just had an electric shock! She then pushed me out the front door to catch the bus to work. When I arrived at the bus stop, Mrs. Ferguson from next door was there and when she saw my hair and my tears she said, What have ye done tae yer hair hen?" I replied between sobs, "It wasnae me Mrs. Ferguson, it was my aunty Betty", to which she replied, "Wait till she gets on her bus (which was on the opposite side of the road) then go back hame an' sort yersel' oot".

After my aunt retired from full time working, she found part-time work in Stirling, and consequently money became very scarce. She had always used to mark jars of some items with a line to tell if it had been used since she last used it. Slices of bread were counted, as were the numbers of biscuits left in a packet and many other items where possible, so of course, this exercise became more intensified. Sometimes I came home from work and Betty would tell me to do myself a boiled egg and toast for my tea. One evening as I was about to sit down and eat, Isobel came in. When she saw this, she was very angry with her mother. My aunt had had a free cooked meal at lunchtime in the canteen where she worked, therefore only required a light meal in the evening. Nevertheless, as my cousin pointed out, I needed a proper meal when I came home from work and that a boiled egg just would not do! Aunty Betty just shrugged her shoulders and replied that I would have what she could afford.

The household and garden chores were leaving me exhausted, but worse than those, I became increasingly lonely. Hamish had changed his job and no longer worked night shift, so I did not see him and Sheena as frequently as I used to do. The only visitors we had was an old friend of my aunt whom she had worked with for many years, who came about two or three times a year, and of course Mr. & Mrs. O'Reilly, likewise a couple of times a year. Isobel was probably the most frequent visitor for her mother, but her grandchildren hardly ever called in, even though they had to pass our house to and from the bus stop. I spent most evenings watching television with my aunt. She did not allow my friends come to the house, although Betty was happy for me to keep in touch with Theresa Lennon, one of my school friends at St. Modan's, most likely because she came from a good Catholic family. Within a two-year period, she came to our house about twice, and when she asked if I would like to baby-sit for an English couple in Causewayhead with her, my aunt happily agreed.

Around this time, I regularly baby-sat for another family a few doors down from us. I enjoyed going down there and, although the children were sometimes a bit of a handful, they were good company. If their mum was going to Bingo, she would pick up the little ornamental Buddha from the top of the television, and kiss its belly for good luck. She was always kind to me and sometimes instead of paying me cash, she allowed me to choose something from clothes that she sold. This would cover a few nights of babysitting. My aunt did not agree with this, but as I had come home with a garment, she would not embarrass herself by making me take it back and ask for cash payment.

At first, I had to give any babysitting money to my aunt, and when Theresa asked me if I would like to accompany her on a holiday to Aberdeen, it was put away each week to pay for it. Mr. & Mrs. Millers' farm also provided extra seasonal income, for example at potato picking time. One day Mrs.

Miller had over paid me by £1, which was a lot of money then, so I told Aunty Betty who sent me back down to the farm to give it back. Mrs. Miller was impressed at my honesty, but I suspect I would not have lost any sleep that night if I had said nothing to either of them. That would definitely have been another one for Father Mac!

When Teresa and I set off for Aberdeen, it was the first time I had been so far away from home without any of the family. I was ecstatic and felt privileged that Teresa had chosen me to accompany her. It was a lovely train journey, which took us through some breathtaking, beautiful scenery. Teresa's pen friend Helen lived on a farm some distance outside Aberdeen, near the town of Ballater, with her parents and older sister. Her parents bred goats whilst her sister was a district nurse. Their house was a typical homely farmhouse and the family were very warm and welcoming. Although it fronted on to a main road, it was surrounded on three sides by fields, with the River Dee flowing through their land at the back. Our accommodation was in the partly converted barn and was lovely and cosy. We ate our meals with the family, which sometimes consisted of fresh trout, caught from the river by Helen's father. Unfortunately, for entertainment, we had to travel into Aberdeen, but the last bus home left the city at 9.30pm, so we did not venture out at night. One day however, after spending the day looking around the city, we went to the cinema to watch the early evening showing of the latest film musical, The Sound of Music. Afterwards, we caught the last bus back to the farm.

A couple of miles along from the farm there was a college for trainee priests called Blair's College. This was the nearest place for local Catholics to attend Mass, so we joined the family and other locals there. The student priests had all gone home for the summer holidays so Teresa and I were invited by the nuns who worked and lived there, to have a look around the college. The two youngest nuns, Sister Mary Raymond and Sister Stella showed us around. The older nuns nick-named them 'those two' because they had a sense of fun and sometimes got into mischief. They took us into a room where they showed us the many different vestments worn by priests on various Holy days such as Saints days, Christmas and Easter. However, the most awe-inspiring vestment was kept in a locked glass cabinet. It was white and was beautifully embroidered with pure gold thread, sewn by Mary Queen of Scots during her imprisonment in Loch Leven castle. Teresa and I couldn't believe our ears when they asked us if we would like to hold it, but we eagerly said yes. When it was handed to me by it's hanger, it was so heavy I almost dropped it on the floor. The historical significance was not lost on me and I felt humbled and privileged to be holding it. I will treasure the memory as long as I live.

On my return home I excitedly told my aunt about the Nuns, the College and the Vestment. She said "Wid ye no like tae become a nun yersel hen?" I replied that I did not think I was good enough, whilst secretly thinking "Oh no! I would miss Top of The Pops!" Since I was not allowed to watch Top of The Pops at home, unknown to my aunt I used to sneak out to watch it wherever I could at various friends' houses. Furthermore, although I had the greatest respect for nuns, and admired their dedication to their work, I had no desire to join them for a life-long career. I was looking forward to a future with a home and family of my own, preferably far away from this one. When Sheena heard this, she said of our aunt, "Huh, she only wants tae sacrifice *you* tae pay fur the past sins o' the rest o' the family!" She was probably right!

Chapter 15

A Guid New Year

Two weeks after my 16th Birthday was New Year, or Hogmanay. I had become friends with a young couple along the road from us, Sally and Tony and occasionally I baby-sat for them. They had asked if I would like to come to their house after 'The Bells' that is, after midnight. Scottish tradition dictates that after midnight and after all the old customs of toasting the new year with the family have been performed, first footing would commence. This usually meant that if you went out around your street and there was a light on in someone's living room and you knocked on their door, you would be invited in to celebrate with good food and a few drinks. After a while, you would move on to someone else's house for more of the same. It was the endeavour of first footers, to set off as soon as possible after the stroke of Midnight to ensure becoming the household's first visitor of the New Year. A piece of coal would be offered to the householder along with the declaration, "Lang may yer lum reek", translated as "Long may your chimney smoke", thus wishing the householder a long life. The householder then invites the first footer inside and offers them the aforementioned food and drink. However, it is widely recognised that there are a number of regional variations to this greeting.

However, this year for the first time, my aunt allowed me to go down the road to Isobel's house to celebrate with her family. She told me not to stay too long as I had to be up early next morning for Mass. Isobel's house was always a happy house on occasions such as this, so I felt very grown-up and excited about going. It turned out to be a memorable 'first New Year' for me, as it was also the first time I had an alcoholic drink. Typical of many households, Isobel had made a huge pan of scotch broth, a steak pie, followed by home baking such as fruitcake, not forgetting the traditional shortbread.

Before arriving at her house, I decided to call in at Sally and Tony's to wish them a Happy New Year. Three or four hours and a huge amount of alcohol later, I was helped home by Moira who had been out searching for me, singing 'A Guid New Year Tae Yin An' All' all the way home. George and Fiona's two children were sleeping in our house that night so aunty Betty could baby-sit for them whilst they too went out to celebrate. Unfortunately, the children were in my bed and heard me getting up in the night to go to the bathroom to be sick. Next morning, New Years Day, I was in the bathroom washing when I heard my aunt's voice calling upstairs. She was about to leave for Mass and instructed me to call in at the newsagent on my way to Church to pay our paper bill. The walk to church was one I had undertaken every week of my life and usually took about 10 to 15 minutes. This walk though, was without doubt, the longest and the hardest by far. I was feeling so ill I even grasped hold of the grass on a slight embankment to stop me from falling over. People were passing and asking if I was all right, at the same time wishing me a Happy New Year! When I walked into the Newsagent, the owner took one look at me and exclaimed "Oh, ye cannae go in tae the chapel lookin' like that, yer aunty Betty'll kill ye"! Then, gently taking me by the shoulders, she took me into the back room and sat me down on a chair. She said her husband would be in soon and that he would run me home in his car. I re-call a feeling of concern coming over me regarding this, because her husband was a retired police officer and I had been drinking whilst under-age! However, I was too ill to worry for too long and the thought soon dispersed, as I was sick in her little backroom sink. When she asked what had caused me to be so sick, I replied that I must have had too much shortbread and cake the previous night! Father Mac was not going to like *this* one! I was slumped in a chair when Patrick, who by this time had left the navy, came in from Mass. He looked at me and said "Whit's wrong wi' you?" but before I could answer, he laughingly exclaimed, "Oh, Aye ken whit's up wi' you"! He then poured a glass of port and told me to drink it, as it would help. "The hair o' the dog" he said. I pushed it away and declared, "No way, I'll never touch anither drop as long as I live"! At that, he walked towards the door saying he was off to Isobel's, because he did not want to be around when our aunty Betty came in. The phrase, lamb to the slaughter, immediately sprang to mind but I was too ill to respond further. The next thing I became aware of was a loud 'BANG', as the back door closed, then 'BANG' again as the kitchen door closed. From the barrage of words and noise, I can only recall, "That wis yer furst an' it'll be yer last". My sentiments exactly, I thought. Usually, such a tirade from my aunt would have me quivering in my shoes, but on this occasion, I could not have cared less. When I could stand her abusive shouting no longer, I headed for the door saying I was going to Isobel's house for some aspirin, as we did not have any. When I walked in the door, Isobel gestured to everyone in the house saying, "Make way everybody, here comes the only person in the world who gets drunk on shortbread and cake"! At that, everyone burst into spontaneous laughter!

Chapter 16

The Green Shoes

Family members who were older than me had a number of places they could go for an enjoyable night out, usually at the weekend. Stirling had two cinemas, The Allan Park and the Regal along with a dance hall called The Plaza. For a short time, there was occasionally dancing in Bannockburn Town hall. Unfortunately, by the time my peers and I were old enough to go to these places, they had begun to close down. Initially to accommodate Bingo halls, but later to make way for a new ring road for the town. Our saving grace came by way of a Discotheque called The Hawaiian Eye which was opened by none other than Jimmy Saville. He was emerging as a very popular Radio Disc Jockey, therefore we were privileged to have him perform the opening. The downside of this disco was that it could only sell non-alcoholic drinks, but sometimes-live bands would appear from as far afield as Glasgow so people came in droves to hear them. Within a few months of opening however, rumours abounded that some people were taking drugs by way of aspirin dropped into the coca-cola of unsuspecting revellers. Of course, a number knowingly partook in this, but to my knowledge, no one openly admitted it. I cannot be sure if it was coincidence, but The Scottish Nationalist Party had won control of Stirling Council, when places for young people to enjoy themselves in the town, begun to disappear. Whatever the reasons, the fact remained that we had to travel further afield to find entertainment. The Museum Hall in Bridge of Allan was nearest then slightly farther was The Silver Dollar in the village of Dollar. The Kinema in Dunfermline, The Raith Ballroom in Kirkcaldy and Doaks' in Falkirk, all became popular venues for the young people from Stirling. Despite their popularity however, it rankled with us that we had to travel so far.

A current fashion item for girls was a crocheted Juliet cap style hat and matching dolly bag (also crocheted with drawstring tie-pulls). As I could crochet, two girls in the Co-op office asked me if I would make these for them when they went to see the famous popular band The Small Faces, who were coming to Doaks' in Falkirk. When I asked my aunt if I could go with them, she said 'No'. It was with mixed feelings of pride and sadness that I watched them board the bus for Falkirk from our living room window, with tears streaming down my face, attired in the hats and bags I had made.

If I wanted to go out to the local Disco on Friday night with my aunt's granddaughter Moira and our friends, I had to ask the weekend before to give aunty Betty time to think about it. Sometimes she would allow me to go but I would have to leave before the others as I was to be home at an earlier time than they. On one occasion when she had said I could not go, it was after tea Friday night before she gave me her decision. Later that evening, Moira came in and asked her granny if she could borrow half a crown or 2/6d. As she was picking up her handbag, she asked what it was for and the reply was, "So I can go tae the Hawaiian Eye". As she handed her the money, my aunt replied, "Ok, here ye go, have a nice time hen"! Although I was disappointed beyond words, I had learned by this time that no amount of protesting or pleading, would alter her decision, therefore I just sat silently fuming, for the rest of the evening! Crying openly would only have infuriated her, therefore tears had to be suppressed and saved yet again for my pillow.

Although I was grown up, and loved pop music and dancing, I have never grown out of my love of football. I was a Glasgow Celtic fan (The Tims) and remain so to this day, although I consider myself a Sheffield Wednesday and Liverpool supporter also. Visits to Celtic Park however had to be covert operations because as with many things, football was out of bounds for me. To see Celtic play a home game we had to travel 26 miles to Celtic Park, in Parkhead, Glasgow. Philomena's husband, along with other members of his family, belonged to the local Celtic supporter's club so they allowed me to go with them. The supporters coach had to pass near our house to pick up others and then go on to the Glasgow road, via Hillpark. We agreed that I should walk up to a pick-up point in Hillpark to meet the coach and that I would be dropped off at the same point on return from the match.

The usual operation went like this. I would tell my aunt that Teresa had invited me to spend the afternoon at her house at the other side of Stirling and, she had asked me to stay for tea. A huge one for Father Mac this time! She liked Teresa so willingly gave her permission. I put on my Celtic supporter's scarf under my coat so that it did not show. Apart from my aunt's disapproval, it was not seemly for a young woman in the 1960s to even like football, let alone be an active supporter of a particular team. Next, came the green and white Juliet hat I had secretly crocheted, which I folded as flat as I could get it, and pushed it deep into my coat pocket. Besides these, my sister had given me her red Tap Dancing shoes and after removing the metal piece from under the toes, I dyed them green. Green shoes were a very unusual sight in the fashion world of the 1960s Stirling. Those colours were usually the reserve of London, but I thought they looked quite impressive. Who knows, perhaps I had started a new trend without realising it! To get the shoes out of the house unseen, I tucked one under each armpit and clenched my upper arms tight against my body. I changed into them on the coach and reversed the procedure during the return journey. It was on this coach, and at the Celtic football ground, where I learned a number of the Irish songs I sing today. The date that is imprinted in my memory however, is 25th May 1967; the day Celtic became the first British football club to win The European Cup. It also happened to be a Holy day of obligation, when Catholics are obliged to attend Mass. I arranged to go to mass in the evening in Stirling with Fiona McCormack, a friend from my school days. As usual, I had to leave the house with my Celtic scarf tucked inside my jacket, and keep it hidden throughout mass, as it was considered disrespectful to wear a football scarf to church. Throughout the service, Fiona and I were itching to go into the town to find out the score and hopefully, celebrate with other Celtic supporters. That evening, we were already singing a victory song some of which went like this…

'It was on the 25th may in far off Lisbon town

The teams were out the stage was set and all the chips were down

The whole world said it was Inter's (Inter Milan) cup

Because they were so strong

But the boys from Paradise were there to prove that they were wrong.

After a couple of other verses where all the players' names were mentioned,

it ended with the words…

They will know us when we meet again,

To sing our battle hymns

The boys who wear the green and white

The Glasgow Celts,

The Tims.'

From that day, the players have been known as The Lisbon Lions. Not long afterwards, I was lucky to obtain all their autographs, along with that of the manager, Jock Stein. It is to my eternal horror and dismay, that through future numerous house moves, they were lost! When Fiona and I emerged from church, we found that Stirling had turned into a ghost town. The streets were empty of traffic and people so Fiona suggested we go to a pub. When we opened the door of the pub at the top of King Street, we were relieved to find what seemed to us, half the population of Stirling, listening to the game on the radio. A huge cheer went up at the full time whistle and Celtic had won 2-1! As the years have passed, I have developed a respect for many football teams, along with individual players and managers alike in the UK, but my heart will always belong to Celtic.

Chapter 17

Freedom

By this time, Patrick had divorced his wife, because of her affair with another man whilst he was away for nine months in Borneo. It had been worrying time for us all, because our forces were out there to quell trouble that had arisen in that country. There was not much news given out publicly then, like there is today regarding Iraq and Afghanistan, so we were very relieved to see him come home safe and sound. Moreover, after his divorce he no longer spent his home leave at the marital home in Bodmin, Cornwall, which meant he came home again to Bannockburn. I was especially pleased to see him back home again, because of his support during the constant unpleasant altercations with our aunt. Furthermore, when I came home from work for lunch, he would have a hot meal ready for me along with some pleasant conversation.

While on one of these home visits, his behaviour had noticeably changed.

At first, it was his drinking habits, and not necessarily, alcohol. This was followed by moodiness and short temper, which were all totally out of character for Patrick. Every time the ice-cream van came round, which was frequent, he would ask me to fetch him two or three bottles of pop. The kettle seemed to be constantly on the boil for tea and, I would frequently walk down to the farm for extra bottles of milk, not just for the tea, but also for him to drink straight from the bottle. Thankfully, his alcohol intake did not appear to increase drastically, but family members had noticed the change in his personality and everyone was becoming very concerned. One day when I had asked him some insignificant question, he responded in an irritable manner with a very sharp "No", which was completely out of character. I later overheard our aunt discussing the incident with Isobel saying, "There must be somthin' wrong wi' him 'cause he even shouted at *her* the day", referring to me.

Before he left to return to Plymouth, uncle Fergus made Patrick promise he would see the navy's medical officer immediately on his arrival. He kept to his word and the next we knew he had phoned our uncle from his hospital bedside, to tell him the medical officer had diagnosed Diabetes. It came as a great relief to us all that at least it was something that could be controlled with daily medication through regular injections, and a carefully monitored diet. The downside however, meant that my brother who so loved the navy, had to be discharged. He had served seven of the nine years that he had originally signed up for and had intended to sign up for life. To say he was heartbroken would be an understatement. He was utterly devastated and even begged them to find him a shore job to enable him to stay in the Navy, but to no avail. With today's advances in the treatment of Diabetes, this would probably be feasible, not so in the 1960s. I was heartbroken too, to see my once so happy brother, so depressed and miserable.

By this time, aunty Sadie and uncle Fergus had moved to a house about ten minutes walk away along the Bannockburn road. Since Sadie did not go out to work, it meant Patrick could live with them so that she could attend to weighing and cooking his food at regular intervals, and generally taking care of him. Uncle Fergus too took an interest in his welfare by encouraging him to return to study, which he did, subsequently winning a place at Edinburgh University where he obtained a degree to become an architect. Given that our uncle was senior architect of a major housing association, during the summer he found Patrick temporary work in his offices in Glasgow, or sometimes the Edinburgh branch. After completing his degree, Patrick joined the firm full time. I was very proud of how he picked himself up, dusted himself down, and made a new career for himself.

Whilst he was living with our aunt and uncle, Patrick regularly popped in to our house to visit aunt Betty and me. One evening however, whilst I was upstairs he and my aunt had a terrible row, during which the teapot went hurtling across the kitchen floor, spilling tea and tea leaves everywhere. On hearing the commotion but not wishing to become embroiled in their argument, I came downstairs and quietly began cleaning up the mess. On seeing me, Patrick exclaimed, "Dinnae you clean that up, let hur dae it, it's time she did some o'her ane cleaning"! He then went on to say to me "Dinnae you worry hen, I'll get you oot o' here one day"! I never did find out what had caused them to argue, but I had never seen my brother so angry and worked up about something, nor had he ever referred to 'getting me out of there' before.

Nevertheless, I *did* get out of there but without any help from my brother, although he was the subject of the argument that had led me to leave.

It happened on a beautiful Sunday in June 1967. Aunty Betty had gone out for the day to the seaside with Isobel and the younger grandchildren. I had cleaned the house, and prepared the evening meal, ready to turn on the cooker later. Patrick had not been in touch regarding an intended visit, so I decided to use the opportunity to visit Philomena and spend some time with her lovely baby girl. I probably stayed longer than I should have because, when I returned later in the evening, I found my aunt had arrived home some time before. She was furious with me for having left the house. Her argument was "What if Patrick had come along and found no one at home", but I strongly suspect that she was angry because I had not stayed in and had *her* evening meal ready for *her* to come home to.

I said I did not want to stay in the house on such a beautiful sunny day, especially as I had done my housework chores, and that Patrick would not have minded if no one had been at home. She would not accept this and began to hit out, slapping my face and hitting me all over. Not until after I had received quite a beating did I retaliate, and even then, I only slapped her on the side of her arm whilst telling her to leave me alone. By now though, I had had enough, so I picked up my basket to leave but she snatched it from me saying I was not taking it as she had paid for it. This was not entirely true for I had paid for half of it. It was a wicker weave basket with a handle crossing over the middle. They were popular at the time and had a patterned, elasticised plastic cover with a slit in the middle, which kept the contents dry when raining, but enabled easy access to the inside. Fortunately, I managed to put my hand inside this slit and retrieve my purse, but had to leave everything else as she continued to beat me as I ran for the door. I have often wondered since that night, what story she told the rest of the family, for who would believe that a woman in her mid 60s could beat up a teenager without injury to herself. Well I can tell you, that is precisely what happened, and furthermore on this occasion, I did not have anything to confess to Father Mac!

As I ran up the footpath, tears streaming down my face, I could hear her calling out "You'll be back, just like the rest of them, you'll be back"! She was of course referring to her son George, my lovely cousin Sheena and my sister Philomena, who had all initially left home after an argument with her. On hearing this remark, I made a promise to myself that I would *never* come back to this house and especially not to her.

I was not consciously aware of where I was heading, but I found myself walking up towards Bannockburn town and out on to the Cowie road to Philomena's house. It was now dark and as the road was unlit, I became a little frightened. However, courage emerged from the anger I was feeling so I removed my shoes, which had a little stiletto style heel and held one in each hand, ready to swipe anyone who came near me intent on causing me harm.

By the time I reached my sister and brother-in-law's house, they and most of the neighbourhood had gone to bed. Rather than risk awakening their baby by knocking on the door, I picked up some loose earth from the garden and threw it at their bedroom window. Philomena was horrified when she saw me. My face was covered in scratches and the blood from them had mingled with my tears, which probably made it look worse than it was.

After telling her what had happened, I said that there was no way I would go back to live with that woman. She agreed and said that first thing in the morning, she would ring the Children's Department and ask someone to come out to see us. The law on fostering in Scotland at that time stated I was under their jurisdiction until I reached the age of 18; it was aged 16 in England; so they had to be involved. Fortunately, the department sent Miss Paterson to speak to us, whom we both found easy to talk with. When we had told her what our lives with our aunt had been like, she wondered why we had not told her years ago. We both replied almost in unison, that if we *had* said anything to her, we would have got a beating as soon as she had gone. Philomena's actual words were "We would have got our backs broken as soon as you had left".

As it was only six months until my 18th Birthday, the Children's Department decided I would not have to go back to my aunt. Subsequently, uncle Fergus collected my clothes from Betty's house along with a few of my personal belongings, and brought them to Philomena's house. My aunt however, did not let me have *all* my things. Missing from my meagre possessions was my prayer book/missal, my rosary beads, and my beautiful pink gold watch that Hamish had bought me from Antwerp. I supposed I had been lucky to come away with the clothes on my back, let alone any of my other belongings. Since Betty would not allow uncle Fergus to use a suitcase, he had to transport every garment in armfuls to his car, even my underwear. The embarrassment did not last long however, as it began to dawn on me that at last, I was free from Aunty Betty and her bullying and controlling family.

Life seemed to improve for me from that night. A real sense of freedom and opportunity swept over me. Nothing, and more especially no one, was going to stop me doing what I wanted to do. I felt confident and happy and when Teresa and I were asked to a party in a house in the nearby village of Fallin: Fallin and Cowie are villages a couple of miles radius from one another. For the first time in my life, at nearly 18 years old, I did not have to ask anyone for permission to go, nor was I told what to wear. I chose to wear a bright yellow shift style dress, which was fashionable at the time, and I thought I looked great. When we arrived, I found that Moira was also invited. Although we did not speak to one another, there was no animosity between us, or so I thought.

During the party, a male friend pulled me up to dance and as he did so, Teresa beckoned to me to leave the room with her. In the hallway she pointed out that there was blood seeping through the back of my dress. We both dashed up to the bathroom where I discovered I had started my period. I was totally unprepared and so as not to cause me any embarrassment, Teresa agreed we should leave and go home. She was staying with me at Philomena's house that night, something aunt Betty would *never* have allowed, so we walked the road from Fallin to Cowie together. It was not too late when we arrived so we found Philomena had not yet gone to bed. When we explained why we were home early, she first laughed, then sympathised with me for missing the party. Next morning however, she received a phone call at work from Isobel. She advised Philomena to put me in a hot mustard bath as soon as she got home from work, because I had gotten up to no good with a bloke at the party. No doubt, a version of events conjured up by Moira. When I heard this, I did not have a clue what she meant so Philomena explained it to me. It had been the practice for generations that if a girl had an unwanted pregnancy, she could induce an abortion by sitting in a hot bath with mustard in it.

I had never heard of anyone who had done this, nor if it was ever successful. Moreover, I found the idea then as now, abhorrent to both my religious and humanitarian beliefs. Philomena's response was brilliant. She told Isobel, whose own daughter had an illegitimate child, that she should sweep her own doorstep before sweeping hers, and then hung up. I did not wish to give any credence to the accusation by becoming further embroiled in a tit for tat slanging match, so I let it rest there. Nonetheless, I was horrified that such a suggestion should come from a so-called respectable, Catholic mother. I was also puzzled that Moira could be party to such a huge, horrible lie; after all, I had never done anything to offend or upset *her*.

A few weeks later, I began nursing training and decided to live-in at the nurse's home. On my days off, I stayed at my sister's house, which gave her mother-in-law some respite from looking after the baby. One day, when my brother-in-law was at home, he made advances and innuendos towards me, which made me very uncomfortable and anxious. Naturally, I told him to leave me alone as I was not even remotely interested and more importantly, reminded him he was married to my sister. He continued to ignore my pleadings, which made my situation intolerable, so when I told my friends Sally & Tony, they suggested I move in with them.

When I informed Philomena that I would be moving out, she asked why. I could not tell her the truth, because I feared that if I did, she would believe her husband and not me. A fear that probably stemmed from the episode of Isobel's missing money. More importantly, her marriage may have stood a better chance of success if I just kept quiet and moved out. I was totally at a loss what to say, so I just said there was no specific reason. She was so angry and frustrated at this that she flew into a rage and beat the living daylights out of me with her slipper, which incidentally, was a fashion mule that had a very hard heel, whilst shouting at me that I would end up just like our mother! Thankfully, Sally came with me to collect my belongings from my sister's house and whilst they were talking in the living room, I was coming downstairs with my suitcase when my brother-in-law stopped me to ask why I was leaving. Huh! He needed to ask! I replied that he knew very well why I was leaving and he was very lucky that I had not told Philomena about him. How ironic then, a year or so later, Philomena left him to live with someone else. The biggest irony though, was she had left behind her little daughter, to be with this man. My sister had walked out on her child, just as our mother had walked out on us years before. I was horrified, and not for the first time in my life, made a solemn oath that I would never abandon any children I might have in the future. Although the baby's father and extended family loved her, and brought her up, it has always been my belief that a baby's place is with its mother. I was also saddened that I never had the opportunity to get to know my niece, nor she me.

So yet again, I found myself leaving home following a beating that I had not deserved. It slowly began to dawn on me, that for most of my life so far, I had been the physical and emotional punch-bag for the frustrations of a number of my mother's family. I vowed never to live, nor have anything to do with, any of them ever again.

Chapter 18

Fond Farewell

During the few short months I lived with Sally & Tony, I found another job where I met the girl who was to become my best and life-long friend. My new place of work was The Kork 'N Seal in Bridge of Allan, a factory where, amongst other things, were made the tops for many famous brands of whisky bottles. Along with the many new friends I met, Lorraine was and still is the best. She introduced me to dance halls and pubs I had never before been to. I was now more liberated than at any other time in my life. Moreover, I was earning more money than I had ever earned before, but better than that, I could decide what to do with it. I was around 18 years old, and hanging out with Lorraine was sheer joy and we had loads of fun. She lived in The Cornton, not far from where I had visited aunty Sadie and uncle Fergus when I was a child. Her family were lovely and to me, normal! Her Mum and Dad both worked, the oldest sibling, a brother, was married, and served in the R.A.F. based at Scampton in Lincolnshire. Her older sister and her mum, worked at the factory alongside us, while her younger sister Jean; who has also remained a life-long friend and confidante, and a stalwart through her Matriarchal role in the family; was at the Riverside Senior School, now Wallace High. Their older sister had a baby called Kimberley who had the most gorgeous head of blonde curls I had ever seen, and we all loved her to bits. Needless to say, she was her Nana and Papa's pride and joy. Further additions to the family over the years have included, amongst others, Lorraine's only daughter Sarah, Jeans only son Brian, and Kimberley's sister Lorraine. The family dog was a beautiful old, black and white collie dog called Monty, whom I loved to bits. He used to howl if we hummed to the tune of Z cars, the television show about police patrol cars.

I began spending more and more time at Lorraine's home, even occasionally spending a full week there, and to my shame and regret, did not offer Sally any board money for that week. This inevitably, led to a full-blown row so Lorraine spoke to her mum and dad, who agreed to have me live with them permanently.

Moving in with Lorraine's family heralded a new phase in my life. It was also the best one so far. I was welcomed into their family with love and warmth. Lorraine's parents treated me like any other member of the family, even when a telling off was necessary. Lorraine recently re-called one evening when she and I were 15 minutes late coming home from a night out, and her Dad carpeted us with a huge telling off before sending us up to bed. Lorraine had said to me "I'm sorry about that" and when I asked, "about what" she replied, "about my Dad shouting at us like that." I said, "Oh no, don't be sorry, at least it shows he cares". I was not used to being shouted at by a caring parent, only by a bullying and domineering aunt, now I could make distinctions between the two.

The factory was only a short distance away, so people from the Cornton who worked there, could walk to and from work. When building work began on a women's prison nearby, a group of Borstal boys were amongst those working there. Lorraine and I used to hear them wolf whistling at us as we passed by, and of course we responded in an appropriate manner. They asked us our names so we replied "Jimmy" and from then on, they would call out "Oh look, here comes the two Jimmy's". It did not help that we also dressed alike. Both had short brown hair, wore beige cord trousers along with red fair isle style jumpers, beige cord shoes, and like everyone else from the factory, wore a blue overall.

Although we went out most weekends, weekday evenings spent at home were enjoyable too because Lorraine's family were great company. Her Dad Derrick was 6ft. 4ins. tall and originally came from Luton. He had met her Mum Rachel who was 4ft. 11ins, whilst he was serving with The Argyll and Sutherland Highlanders based at the Raploch Barracks near Stirling, during the war. He was very funny and could easily make us all laugh, but at the same time, could be a strict disciplinarian, who kept us all on our toes. Her mum was the sweetest natured woman I had ever known. She played the piano and the accordion, and sang too. She worked hard at her full-time job in the factory, would help anyone if she could, and always had a lovely cheery smile. We all paid our board or dig money to her on Friday, but by Monday we were borrowing it back again. It would not surprise me if she never actually gained financially from our contribution to the household at all! She was a very popular woman at work and in the community, and over forty years later, I have still not met her equal. Sadly, Rachel and 'Big Dick' have passed away, but if there really is a place called heaven, that is where you will find Rachel.

Lorraine's uncle John, her mother's brother, lived on the same street with his wife aunty Mary, and children Joan, Alexis, Christine, Jacqueline, Harry, and Fiona. They were a smashing family and I used to love visiting their house. They reminded me of Isobel's younger children, whom I missed terribly. Aunty Mary is every bit as sweet as Rachel was, so too is Alexis and her husband Pat. I love meeting up with them at family weddings, etc.

Although we sometimes went out on Friday night, it was Saturday night we looked forward to most. Saturday daytime was usually spent shopping for clothes, make-up etc. This was especially exciting for me, considering Aunty Betty did not allow me to wear make-up. Afterwards we called in at the café on Barnton Street in Stirling town centre to catch up with friends and general gossip. The Stirling Arcade provokes happy memories too. The lovely shops and even a pub proved popular with our generation. It was a great place to shelter when caught out in a rain shower and in the early evenings, there was always a boy or girl waiting or hoping, for their 'date' to arrive. An old gypsy or travelling woman called Mrs Johnstone used to sit begging in the Arcade wrapped up in so many tartan blankets that only her tiny little head popped through. She was always polite and grateful when we dropped a coin or two into her lap, but despite never bothering anyone, she was moved away by a police officer, only to return a short while later.

Mini-skirts and high-heeled platform shoes were the fashion of the day. My aunt would have had a fit if she had seen me wearing any of those fashion statements. That was the difference in Lorraine's family household. Her parents did not object to us wearing fashionable clothes, within reason of course. We never wore anything too outrageous, nor did anything we were ashamed of, we were just ordinary teenagers having fun. Our taste in music varied, but our favourite at that time was Tamla Motown, a music label and sound consisting of mainly Black artistes from the U.S.A. The Four Tops, Temptations, Diana Ross and the Supremes, Otis Redding, Marvin Gaye, to name just a few. Tamla Motown had a great distinguishing sound of its own and was very popular throughout the U.K. Besides these we loved most of the British bands too. The Small Faces, The Herd; A Peter Frampton poster held pride of place, full length behind our bedroom door; Amen Corner, Spencer Davis Group, to name just a few again. The Dobbie Hall in Larbert and Doaks' in Falkirk were our favourite dance hall venues, especially after The Hawaiian Eye closed down. The Allan Park became Stirling's only cinema after The Regal closed. I much preferred the Regal because I thought it had a more comfortable atmosphere and it had a good restaurant too. The Gateway Bar was a popular venue to meet up with friends over a drink and sometimes a live band appeared there. The American Bar behind The Station Hotel was popular too, as was the golden Lion Hotel on King Street.

Nevertheless, Stirling was still without sufficient places for the young population to let their hair down. A number of young people had already left to live in England and more followed. Manchester and Sheffield were popular destinations and a number of girls from the factory had moved there. Strangely, I do not re-call anyone moving as far as London, and after all, that was *the* place to be in the 1960s in the whole of Europe. Perhaps that would have been too big a step to take for us provincial town girls.

Finding employment was not a problem, as this was still the era when a person could leave a job on Friday and begin a new one on Monday. Whilst living at Sally & Tony's, I had met Tony's brother Andy who lived in Sheffield. When he visited, he told Lorraine & I what a great place Sheffield was. The friendly people, good jobs with wages to match, and most importantly for us, at that time, the wonderful night-life. Fashionable clothing too was more liberating in Sheffield than in Stirling. Tony had said that no matter what you wore, no one batted an eye. In Stirling however, you were not 'cool' if you did not wear the current single fashion 'must have'.

Lorraine and I had been pondering over what Andy told us about Sheffield, when we heard that a girl at the factory who had gone to live there, was looking for a new flat-mate. She had kept in touch with me and asked if I was interested in moving south to join her. Although Stirling was beginning to move forward within the fashion and music world, sharing a flat with friends was still unheard of. What may have been considered unacceptable by our Scottish parent's generation, was definitely 'cool and acceptable' by us. After discussing it with Lorraine, we agreed that I should take up the invitation and Lorraine would follow whenever another vacancy arose. Although Lorraine's parents did not want me to go; we had not told them at this point of Lorraine's future intention; they respected my decision and told me I was welcome in their home whenever I liked. However, her Dad had always said, "When you make your own bed you lay in it." His words were still ringing in my ears when I waved good-bye to Lorraine at Glasgow Central railway station that July day, and began the journey, which subsequently led to that 'Sheffield Landing'.

The proverbial bed he referred to turned out to be no bed of roses, but I had made that bed myself, without help or hindrance from anyone else. Many more trials and tribulations were to emerge throughout the rest of my life, but at last I was truly independent. Sheffield was, and still is in my opinion, a beautiful City. In the 1960's, it was awarded the title of 'The Greenest Industrial City in Europe'. Beautiful breathtaking countryside is only 15 minutes from the city centre, similar to that in The Trossachs. I formed a great social network of friends with whom I enjoyed pubbing and clubbing. I became involved in the Trade Union movement where amazingly, my opinion not only mattered, but also was asked for. Shopping for and wearing fashionable clothes, was a new Utopia! I visited Scotland and Lorraine's family regularly, and then a year later she, along with our friend Louise, joined me in Sheffield. More importantly however, I had left behind my mother's family, and could look forward to the future building a family of my own!

Printed in Great Britain by
Amazon.co.uk, Ltd.,
Marston Gate.